Molly

Monkey Mischief at Twycross Zoo

Molly Badham and Nathalie Evans

with Maureen Lawless

POCKET
BOOKS

LONDON · SYDNEY · NEW YORK · TOKYO · SINGAPORE · TORONTO

First published in Great Britain by Simon & Schuster UK Ltd, 2000
This edition first published by Pocket Books, 2002
An imprint of Simon & Schuster UK Ltd
A Viacom Company

1 3 5 7 9 10 8 6 4 2

Simon & Schuster UK Ltd
Africa House
64–78 Kingsway
London WC2B 6AH

www.simonsays.co.uk

Simon & Schuster Australia
Sydney

A CIP catalogue record for this book is available
from the British Library

ISBN 0-7434-0908-6

Typeset in ITC Garamond by SX Composing DTP, Rayleigh, Essex
Printed and bound in Great Britain by
Omnia Books Ltd, Glasgow

This book is dedicated to our many Zoo friends and
associates who have helped us over the years and
particularly the Zoo staff past and present

Contents

CHAPTER ONE

Old Friends and Monkey Business

It is spring, and pale sunshine dapples my bedroom window as I lie awake and wait for our dawn chorus to begin. The muted high-pitched whooping of a Pileated (crested) Gibbon sets off the rest of his group, but is soon overtaken by the deeper tones of the nearby large black Siamang Gibbons; the noise they emit from their throat sacs booms out like drums across the landscape. In the distance a tiger yawns a growl and the squawking of macaws swells the familiar chatter which daily greets the rising sun.

A new day has begun. It is time to start preparing for some of the half a million visitors who visit Twycross Zoo in the heart of Leicestershire each year, eager to see the apes and rare monkeys, the chimps and orangs, elephants and giraffes who have become our main attractions.

Keepers are already arriving to start the early morning feeding; other staff – groundsmen, curators, maintenance workers and café staff – will soon join them. Downstairs our two dogs are barking a greeting to the administration staff as they invade the office at the rear of the house.

Over breakfast my business partner, friend and companion for the last fifty years, Nathalie Evans and I discuss our plans for the day. My first call is always a visit to our oldest inhabitants, the chimps, some of whom have been with us for over thirty years. Every morning Nat makes three buckets of tea ready for the moment I set off for the complex close to the house to take my old friends their morning tea and biscuits.

Three of the chimps were born at the zoo and brought up in the house. Flynn, Becky and Josie are already awake and waiting for their breakfast treats as I enter their kitchen through the safety door, closing it behind me before passing through the inner door which leads to their heated bedplaces. The three chimps now live in the old Gorilla House where they have four bedplaces, two inside day quarters and an outside enclosure with play equipment. Inside their house is a sunken bath which is filled with warm water during the summer so they can enjoy splashing around the edge and fill plastic containers which they empty over the floor.

In the winter when it snows they have another favourite diversion. They collect handfuls of snow and bring it into their house to place on the heated floor, then watch it melt – and never fail to be astounded as it disappears before their eyes.

Their other source of entertainment is a television set which they watch when there are no visitors to amuse them. Their favourite programmes are horse racing, boxing matches and wildlife documentaries. They do *not* appreciate newsreaders, operatics or cookery programmes – perhaps the latter are boring because the chimps only like raw fruit and vegetables. Flynn is now twelve years old, a mature chimp who could be considered dangerously powerful, except that he has never forgotten our close relationship in his early days or the tricks he loved to perform which entertained him as much as ourselves.

Every morning he searches amongst his bedding to find a present which he holds in his strong stubby fingers before handing it to me. It might be a piece of paper, an old chocolate wrapper or a bit of cloth, but it is his gift to me, a sign of friendship. Sometimes he will put one finger through the bars and hand me a piece of paper so that I can wrap it around his finger like a bandage – reminiscent of the time he cut himself and had to wear a plaster.

Thirteen-year-old Josie and twelve-year-old Becky keep their distance, standing a few feet away in the rear, anticipating Flynn's annoyance if they attempt to get their tea first or have first choice of which jug they will drink from. Given the option of red, blue, or white, the first choice of all of them would be the red jug.

It seems universal that red is a chimp's favourite colour, and as usual it is Flynn who takes the red jug and concentrates on drinking his tea while I hand the others theirs and begin to dole out the biscuits, keeping a wary eye on Flynn to prevent him rushing over to steal those of his two female companions. A firm 'No!' still has the desired effect, even though he has the strength to knock all of us out of the way if he chose.

Instead he takes my outstretched hand and walks with me into a corner where he sits down, his brown eyes smiling in anticipation as I take a chocolate bar from my pocket and balance it on his head and repeat the words so familiar to him: 'Good boy, don't move,' and he sits as still as a statue until I take the chocolate off his head and hand it to him.

People who think that teaching chimps and monkeys to perform tricks is demeaning them should tell that to the chimps. They just adore learning new skills and love to show them off to an audience. Today, Flynn has an audience of just three, but the pleasure it gives him to perform is blatant. He chuckles and beams when Becky, Josie and I applaud loudly.

Then it is he who holds out his hand, which I take, and he stands waiting for me to point to one of his feet, at which he lifts it slowly into the air and stands holding it in his hand like a misshapen ballet dancer. Bravo! His performance complete, the trio know exactly what is coming next and start to clap when I present them with an assortment of clothes – the red jumpers and cardigans they adore, although any thick woollies whatever the colour are given a grunt of approval, while trousers, knickers and bras keep them happy for many hours trying them on. No painstaking hours have been spent teaching them to don the clothes; all of the primates love to dress up, hence the constant supply of garments collected from jumble sales and charity shops, each item having had its zips and buttons removed to ensure they are not swallowed by an experimenting chimp.

I leave them happily engrossed in deciding which outfit they will wear for the day. In Becky's case she seems to have plumped for an old pair of large pink silk knickers – having managed to force the whole of her body into one leg of them to parade proudly around the house in a perfect parody of a catwalk model.

The chimp quarters opposite are my next port of call. These are sometimes referred to as the 'geriatric wards' as they house some of the old-timers, and the older chimps are already waiting impatiently for my arrival. As they hold their hands out for their jugs of tea and biscuits, memories always flood back. There is Joli, who amazed everyone with her aptitude for painting and who was more than happy to display her artistic talents when wildlife artist David Shepherd came to call.

Greeting me now is Vicky, one of five chimps who went down with pneumonia when they were very young and had to be put in oxygen tents in our house until they recovered.

Jambo, who is now eighteen years old, has sadly lost his hair and is completely bald, so that when he rushes from one side of his house to the other he looks like a streaker! All kinds of veterinary and herbal treatments have been tried, as well as experiments with his diet, but there has been no real improvement even though Jambo is bathed at fortnightly intervals with a special shampoo and dressed with skin ointment which keeps his skin supple and avoids sores. He takes it all in his stride and his mate Tojo does not seem to mind his strange looks.

Like many of our chimps, Tojo was hand-reared after being caught in the wild and rescued by some friends who were on holiday in Africa. They were horrified to see the tiny chimp, only about twelve months old, being teased by native children who were sitting around a bonfire throwing hot ashes at her. They bought her for £10 and smuggled her under their coats to another friend, who managed to arrange a flight to England for her and a permanent home at Twycross.

When she arrived she was very frightened and we had to gain her confidence, bottle-feeding her in the house; even then it took her years to regain her confidence in human beings.

Other chimps have been wild caught; often their mothers have been shot by hunters and the babies sold for hard cash – a trade which has encouraged further slaughter of the chimpanzee population.

Every time I walk into the building and see the plaques with their names and dates of birth, a feeling of satisfaction overwhelms me. All of these chimps have a chequered history; many have been hand-reared and because of their background cannot be integrated to live within a group, but they do strike up friendships and live in pairs. Melody, our oldest surviving chimp who has achieved the grand age of forty-two, is obsessed with nail varnish and loves nothing better than to peel it off if I put my hand out to her.

Choppers, who is now twenty-eight years old, and her friend Noddy who is three years older, were both wild caught and rescued by Mrs Locke from Nairobi who then presented them to the zoo. Noddy has given birth to four babies, three boys and a girl, and Choppers has had just one daughter. They are both living examples of how much we have progressed since the early days, when any ape or monkey was lucky to survive longer than a few years because of our ignorance.

One of my favourites, because she is so unusual and attractive, is Coco – nicknamed 'The Girl with the Tan'. While most chimpanzees in the wild and at Twycross are black, there are a small minority of the species, like Coco, who are pale brown. In some old Natural History books there was mention of sightings of chocolate-coloured or brown chimps, but the first one we saw in the flesh was Coco, a stunningly beautiful chimp with tangerine skin and hair the colour of Cadbury's chocolate bars.

Coco was born in Africa and at an early age had been adopted by the military in Senegal as their mascot, although she was so popular and spoiled by the soldiers that she was almost a pin-up. Then, as she matured and no longer had a baby face and was beginning to assert herself, the military command decided that she was too disruptive and would have to be moved on. Not such an easy task to find a home for yet another chimp but eventually they contacted us and we agreed to take her, a chocolate chimp, a mutation of her species.

The flight was booked and she arrived early one morning at Heathrow Airport where we were waiting to transport her back to Twycross. Despite her attractive looks she was tired and bewildered by the long journey and did not know anyone, and even worse, did not *want* to know any of us.

After a few days, when Coco had begun to settle, her shyness gave way to her true nature. It was obvious that she had been teased by the soldiers, for if she didn't get her own way she would fly into a tantrum and bite the hand that fed her. Her reaction showed the lack of trust she had in humans and this made us sad. Eventually we found her a companion of her own age which gave her more confidence, but despite being beautiful to look at, with her unique colouring, she is still of uncertain temperament.

I am delighted to report that, some time after she joined us, Coco mated with a black male chimp called Oscar and produced another chocolate chimp, founding a dynasty of brown chimps, including her granddaughter, Mcwendu, who was born at Twycross in 1993.

During my visits to the chimps I see many old friends beginning to show their age, but their welcome always brings back a wealth of happy memories, of nursing them through illness, helping to rear many of their babies, gaining their confidence and forging everlasting bonds. Looking at them I never cease to wonder at the part they have played in my life or the circumstances which led two rival pet-shop owners to start one of the most interesting collections of zoo animals and become recognised experts in primates.

I will never forget the day in 1949 that I stood outside *Bunny's Pet Shop*, which was owned by my arch rival Nathalie Evans, entranced by the small furry monkey whose hair was a soft, smoky grey and whose bright brown eyes gazed into mine through the window. I had no idea then that this monkey was the catalyst that would hurtle us into untold adventures changing our lives for ever. I knew only that he was the most beautiful creature I had ever seen, and even though I could not afford the £35 he cost *I had to have him*.

So great was my desire to possess this lovely monkey that I overcame any qualms I had in entering the shop of my competitor to give her business which I could ill afford. It had been a bitter blow when Nathalie had opened her shop in opposition to my own *Wellworth Dog Shop* in Sutton Coldfield, Birmingham. It was hard enough to make a living with people still suffering from the aftermath of a war which left everyone impoverished – and all the more hurtful because Nathalie and I had struck up our friendship in the late 1930s when we met at the local riding school. We both kept our own horses at livery there, and had spent a lot of time together horse riding and showing our dogs.

At first I found it hard to accept that we were now not only rivals in the show ring but also in business. It was in the days of rationing, of limited coupons to buy clothing, food and petrol and in the end it was the latter that forced me to overcome any feelings of hostility. If we were to continue to be able to take our dogs to shows as well as make deliveries from the shops, it seemed sensible to share our meagre petrol allowance and resume our friendlier rivalry.

In one respect Nathalie had already stolen a march on me. While I concentrated on supplying dogs, cats, and petfood, Nat kept a whole range of pets – from budgies and parrots, kittens and puppies, to the more exotic in the form of all kinds of small monkeys. There was always a crowd of people gazing into her shop window being entertained by the antics of these mischievous and unusual animals, and I was no exception. From the moment I caught sight of that one monkey I was hooked.

Oddly enough, my decision to have him helped to bury our rivalry and cemented our friendship for ever. We now shared another passion – an abiding interest in apes and monkeys and their welfare.

When I handed over my money for that first monkey I had no idea what kind of monkey he was or where he came from. Even when I learned that he was a Humboldt's Woolly Monkey from South America it meant nothing to me, but from that moment a lifetime love affair with monkeys and primates began – together with a continuing learning process spanning half a century.

I called my new acquisition Sambo and immediately he took over my life. He was about twelve months old and the size of a three-month-old kitten. From the beginning I felt a great affinity with him and recognised that here was an animal of superior intelligence to the dogs and cats I was used to, and I was fascinated by his ability to learn and communicate.

He house-trained himself, using the paper in his cage as a litter tray, and went everywhere with me, his silvery-grey tail wrapped tightly around my waist. He was totally demanding, hating to be separated from me for even a few minutes. When I put him back in his cage he would scream and scream until I gave in and went back for him. He slept in my bedroom in his cage and when he got bolder would follow me into the bathroom and climb into the bath to splash about in the water. My dachshunds accepted him quite readily even though they now took second place to him, and my Siamese cat would spend hours washing him all over.

Everything about Sambo was a delight; his love of the clothes my friends knitted for him which he gloried in wearing and his babyish dependence and the affection he showed to me.

Today I would recognise immediately that he was not a well animal because Woolly Monkeys only make delightful pets while they are babies or if they are sickly. Compared to our colony of Woolly Monkeys at the zoo who are strong, healthy and energetic, Sambo was very frail, but in my ignorance I thought his clinging dependence just a lovable habit.

I was thirsty to learn everything about Woolly Monkeys and devoured all the books and scientific papers written about them and primates. I learned that they live in the treetops 150 feet high above the South American jungle and eat seedpods, fruit and nuts.

Following the instructions I had been given about his diet to the letter, I fed him on apples, bananas, oranges and grapes. Initially he seemed to thrive but it was an age of ignorance when even London Zoo knew little about keeping exotic species and they, like the author of the diet sheet, overlooked two necessary ingredients in a monkey's diet if they are to remain healthy: protein, which in the wild they would find in insects, birds' eggs, and even birds themselves and other small creatures – and lots of fresh air.

It was summer and I would often take my little friend for drives in the car. Like most monkeys he just adored it, lying across my shoulders staring at the passing cars while I relished the startled looks of the other drivers who inevitably did a double-take at my unusual passenger.

Times with Sambo were good, but business was bad so Nat and I decided to add another string to our bow to try to improve our finances. We bought a caravan and on

Sundays we would set off with it to dog shows, using it not only as accommodation but as a trade stand from which to sell petfoods, collars and leads and other pet accessories. With the caravan as our base, we could enter our dogs in the show ring as well as increase our income. The dachshunds came with us and so did Sambo, who would not normally be allowed to go into dog shows but could stay inside the caravan and could play quite happily out of sight of the show officials.

That autumn of 1949, business was at its slackest so we decided to take Sambo and the dogs for a caravan holiday at Blackpool. I think that was the time he was most happy, out on the grass in the fresh air, playing with a ball amongst the bushes. Watching him and laughing at his tricks, we were blissfully ignorant that the diet I was feeding Sambo was slowly helping to kill him and that already he had only three short months to live.

Back home, with winter approaching and the temperature already dropping, I became increasingly worried about how Sambo, whose natural habitat was a hot humid rainforest, would cope with an English winter. I sought expert advice from London Zoo and was told that he would only survive if he was kept in a temperature of 80 degrees Fahrenheit and not allowed to get cold. I took the advice without question, not knowing that in those days even London Zoo had not succeeded in keeping South American monkeys alive for any length of time.

As the days grew colder Sambo was installed in my bedroom with the gas fire burning day and night at full blast. I could hardly bear the heat and suffered sleepless nights but put up with it because I thought it was keeping Sambo alive. I was wrong. It was heartbreaking to see him picking at his food, eating less and less, and becoming weaker and fading away before our eyes. Even the vet had no answer, because at that time no one realised the tremendous deficiency South American monkeys were suffering through our ignorance.

When Sambo died I felt as though my world had fallen

apart and I blamed myself for his death. The first few days after he had gone seemed so empty. My whole life had revolved around my tiny friend, my social life was nil, my outlook had narrowed to an almost obsessive interest in monkeys and primates and I could not imagine life without one.

Nathalie shared my grief at losing Sambo and also my resolve that, despite constant financial worries as profits from both shops began to plummet, we would take in more monkeys and increase our knowledge until we could give them a happy, healthier and longer life.

CHAPTER TWO

Our Delinquent Chimp

It was Nathalie, practical as ever, who suggested that she close her shop and that we pool our resources and go into partnership in my shop in Station Road, Sutton Coldfield. This, she reasoned, should bring in enough income for us to pursue our abiding interest in exotic species.

We saved more expense by moving into the flat over the shop, which was a grand Victorian building with spacious rooms, high ceilings and ornate cornices. The large windows were the perfect showcase in which to display African Green Monkeys and Capuchin Monkeys, which drew avid crowds. In particular, the children were entranced; they would stand, noses pressed against the glass, their eyes wide with wonder at these strange creatures. They persisted in dragging their parents along on Sundays to see our latest offerings and we were rewarded by a satisfying increase in trade.

Their favourites were always the Capuchin Monkeys, the diminutive creatures they had read about in books who, dressed in little tunics, would accompany the organ grinders, holding out a bowl to collect pennies from appreciative audiences. One of our Capuchins' favourite tricks was to get a couple of coins and clap them down on a hard surface in time to music, to the delight of the crowds who gathered on the pavement outside the shop to watch their antics. Already we had begun to realise just how different each species of monkey was, both physically and in their temperament and abilities. The little Capuchins were far more intelligent and better-tempered than the African Green Monkeys. They were always eager to learn new skills and, with their beautiful little hands, were extremely dexterous, easily undoing any nut or bolt – a task far too advanced for an African Green Monkey.

Our fascination for monkeys soon came to the attention of the dealers in exotic animals. They regarded us as two eccentric, gullible women who let their hearts rule their heads, and who were soft enough to buy a blatantly sick animal to try to save its life. They welcomed us with open arms and were constantly on the telephone, tempting us with yet another type of monkey to add to our collection.

In those days we were indeed two susceptible women in a man's world, hacking our way through the jungle of dodgy dealers and pathetic backstreet pet shops where we laid out money for monkeys who lay sick and shivering in their own excreta. Although we knew instinctively we could not save them, at least Nat and I could give them some comfort, good food and cleanliness in their last months.

At that time, animals were not protected from human predators; they were captured in the wild and shipped by boat to Europe, often suffering deprivation and death en route. As one batch of animals suffered and died, they were replaced by other ill-fated creatures. These were the days, too, of travelling menageries, when lions and tigers were transported in cramped cages to live out their short lives in misery; of circuses where animals were bullied into performing tricks for an uneducated public.

A decade before television discovered David Attenborough, wildlife programmes and conservation, the general public queued to see real-life tigers, lions, bears, chimps and gorillas, increasing the demand for even more exotic creatures to be snatched from their natural habitat.

However, many zoo visitors left disillusioned and disturbed by the conditions in which they found the animals: the cramped, barred cages, where creatures were imprisoned in solitary confinement, bare concrete runs where former lords of the jungle now paced mindlessly from side to side. It was pitiful to see these magnificent animals in such appalling conditions. Our own visits to these awful places made us realise that only respectable zoos with a scientific approach and backing would help us gain more knowledge about the welfare of monkeys.

London Zoo became a Mecca for us in our thirst for information which would improve the health and well-being of our own small collection. It was there we saw the species of apes which would take over the rest of our lives.

One warm summer's day, Nat and I stood amongst a crowd of people and saw our very first chimps' tea party. I was fascinated as I watched the young chimps dressed like children sitting in their chairs, the hairy hands nimbly lifting cups to their lips and passing plates, obviously enjoying every minute as much as the onlookers. I looked at Nathalie and as our eyes met I knew that she had felt the same excitement as me; here was an animal with whom we could really communicate and with the intelligence and skill to be taught like a child.

The thought of being able to create such a bond and unlock the potential that was undoubtedly there was a mind-blowing prospect. From that moment we were determined to have a chimp of our own.

It was 1951 and even though there were no controls on the importation of chimps they were relatively scarce, as we discovered when we scoured dealers and zoos all over the country to satisfy our passionate desire to acquire a chimpanzee. Zoos were polite but decidedly disapproving, viewing us as just two more foolish people wanting a chimp as a pet – a not unreasonable assumption as we later learned when we were inundated with unwanted chimps whose owners could not cope with their antics.

Refusing to be daunted, we continued our search until one day we found a dealer who had just the one female chimp for sale. We were so excited that instead of waiting until we found the right specimen, we threw caution to the winds and bought her sight unseen. After all our previous disappointments with sick monkeys, warning bells should have rung loudly when the dealer casually mentioned that she did have a bit of a cold, but such was our enthusiasm we dismissed any doubts that might have crept into our minds.

We couldn't wait for her arrival, but our joy was short-lived when a very sick animal arrived with a streaming cold, which rapidly turned into bronchitis. We comforted ourselves with the thought that nursing her through her illness would forge a strong bond and for a time that seemed to be the case as Sue, as we christened her, responded to our ministrations with great affection.

Like Sambo, she clung to me and wanted constant attention, which she repaid by being loving and demon-strative. It was only when she began to feel better that we realised we not only had a tyrant on our hands but one who had the intelligence to be as manipulative as a spoilt child.

She demanded constant attention and as long as we gave in to her every whim she was happy; if we dared to ignore her she would fly into a rage. When we tried to put her back in her cage while Nat or I attended to the shop she would scream and make messes; only if we devoted every waking moment to her would she behave. We rapidly learned that we were dealing with a creature of considerable intelligence who could size up situations and our weaknesses and take advantage of both.

Because of her physical strength and willpower, there was no way we could force Sue to do anything she didn't want to. As with a wayward child, we had to give her things to occupy her mind, and because she so much resembled a human child we began to treat her like one. When she came to us she could already drink from a cup. Now we bought her a high chair like a baby and sat her at the table and taught her to feed herself.

Sue loved learning, and after observing us intently at breakfast she learned how to use a spoon to eat boiled eggs as neatly as we did, delicately dipping her spoon in the salt and pepper, picking up her bread and butter soldiers and dunking them in her egg. She could also pour out tea without spilling a drop and her table manners were impeccable. She shared our food and had her own special favourites including asparagus, which she adored. Sue would have been at home at any sophisticated dinner party as she dipped the asparagus tips into butter before transferring them carefully to her mouth to savour every mouthful.

Unwittingly, by teaching Sue table manners and allowing her to eat with us and share the same food, we were supplying her with the vital protein and vitamins which our other monkeys had been lacking. It was the breakthrough which not only stimulated her mind but also helped her to grow into a strong, healthy chimp.

Her development was astonishing and she learned to be house-trained far quicker than most toddlers. At first we dressed her in nappies and rubber pants before training her to use a child's potty. From that she progressed to using the lavatory and would always pull the chain afterwards. Even when she sat with us watching television, which she loved to do, she would suddenly drag herself off the settee and rush to the bathroom to spend a penny, then return to carry on viewing.

Undoubtedly Sue was an exceptional chimp, and due to the amount of time we spent with her she could achieve a higher potential than other chimps who did not have the same benefits.

By the time she was a few months older and weighed 30 lbs it was almost impossible to persuade Sue to go back into her cage, so we hit on another distraction which worked very well and also increased her physical well-being. Each day we would drive her in the car to Sutton Park, whose 2,500 acres of beauty spot stretch alongside the perimeter of the town, and let her run loose amongst the greenery, bracken and trees which provided her with a natural playground. It was here that Sue came into her own, swinging from branch to branch with the natural agility of a chimp in the wild and loping alongside us across the grass.

On these excursions we dressed her in children's clothes, not to parody a human child but for the very practical reason of keeping her warm – another unwitting step in our learning curve that was steering us more by luck than judgement to the realisation that monkeys and chimps do not have to be kept constantly in hothouse conditions. Given the right clothing, they can adapt to any temperature, be it in Africa, Aylesbury or the Antarctic.

Dressing her in clothes also provided another entertainment for Sue, and anyone who criticises dressing up chimps has obviously never witnessed the enormous pleasure they get from their clothes and how individual they are in their preferences for different items of clothing. Sue adored her shoes, which she would fetch and hand to us when she felt it was time for her daily trip to the park. And she developed a new skill in learning to dress herself.

Nat and I found willing help at a local shop called Longmore's. After the salesgirls' initial surprise at being asked to dress a young chimp, they joined in enthusiastically to help find the right outfits, with Sue conveying her own preferences just like any other fashion-conscious child. Bright colours like red, orange and yellow were her favourites, and anything drab was immediately thrown aside.

Of course, we had some very strange looks when passers-by saw us leaving our shop for Sue's daily jaunt or when they caught a glimpse of her wrinkled face peeking at them through the car window.

We did keep her on a lead for part of the time in the park, but when the coast was clear we would let her off so that she could climb and swing from branch to branch and tree to tree with an exuberance that lightened our hearts.

There she was in her element, a chimp doing what came naturally, but she always wanted to include us in her games, one of which was to hold our hands so that we could swing her round and round. One day we were so absorbed in this game that we failed to see a woman observing us disapprovingly. We only knew of her presence when she strode over and shouted, 'How dare you swing a child by the arms like that!'

At the sound of her voice Sue turned to look at her, opening her lips and showing her teeth in what could be interpreted as a smile or a threat. The woman's eyes almost popped out as she backed off and made a hasty exit saying, 'Oh, my God, it's a monkey.'

Like a child, when the time came for her to return home Sue would ignore our calls. High above us on a branch she would turn a deaf ear and no amount of calling would move her. In the end we used 'child psychology' and turned and walked away towards the car, which brought her scrambling down from the tree to rush after us.

These daily trips had the desired effect of tiring her out and for the next few hours until closing time she would happily go into her cage, giving us some respite to concentrate on our business.

As Sue became more accustomed to her trips to the park she also became more demanding. If we were downstairs in the shop attending to a customer and were a few minutes late in shutting up to take her out, she would thump so violently on the floor of the flat above that she would shake the plaster off the ceiling.

When we first moved into the flat we had been driven mad by our one neighbour who played classical music at a deafening pitch and whose wife sang aria after aria from numerous operas in a loud but out-of-tune voice. In desperation we had built a false wall between them and us, filling the cavity with bag after bag of sawdust which drowned her out. Now when Sue decided to have one of her tantrums we were thankful we had been driven to take this measure.

Boredom was our biggest enemy and Sue became bored very easily. As fast as we provided her with toys to distract her and taught her more skills, she would tire of them and become bad-tempered – when her only answer was to wreck the nearest things at hand.

We bought her a bike and a scooter but she soon mastered them and wanted something else to take up her attention.

On an inspiration we bought her a child's sewing set and she would spend hours with a darning needle and pieces of wool, laboriously stitching away. It was one of her favourite occupations. We then purchased a carpentry set, probably one of our more ridiculous ideas, as Sue quickly learned to hammer nails into pieces of wood, which she did with gusto before turning her energies to the hand drill with which she would drill holes; firstly in blocks of wood and then in everything in sight, including drilling a hole through the carpet and the floorboards and through the shop ceiling.

Needless to say, Sue's woodworking activities were not appreciated and the hammer and drill were confiscated, which caused another furore of anger, prompting her to vent her disapproval by indulging in one of her favourite destructive occupations – removing the plaster radiants from our gas fires and crunching them up. We did sometimes wonder whether they contained some mineral which was deficient in her diet, but whatever the reason we did not have a complete gas fire left in the flat.

Entertaining her in the evenings was simple – we just gave her a bath. Like most chimps, Sue loved water, and splashing around in the bath and soaping herself all over provided her with endless amusement as well as keeping her spotlessly clean.

Because of Sue, our circle of friends became quite limited. Although she loved us, the only other person she would tolerate was our postwoman, Renee Carley, whose love of animals matched our own. Renee had instant empathy with Sue and the other monkeys and because of this we were lulled into the belief that our mischievous chimp would be friendly to everyone else. We were proved very wrong when another friend who had heard all about Sue came to our flat to see her. The meeting was over in seconds when Sue took an instant dislike to the stranger entering her territory and bit her so badly that she had to be taken to hospital to have her hand stitched.

Our social life went into a definite decline. Even though Sue was locked in her cage on the rare occasions we had visitors to dinner, it did not go down well when we had to ask them if they would mind eating their meal in the bedroom while Sue joined us at the dining table as was her custom.

It reflected her domination and our devotion to her that we were willing to sacrifice friendships to keep her happy, although sometimes we did feel that perhaps we had taken on more than we had bargained for.

Any fleeting thoughts of parting with her were dispelled when without warning Sue became ill, constantly vomiting and running a high temperature. We were totally mystified and with the general lack of knowledge about primates felt totally unable to help her. Veterinary surgeons had no experience of primates and there were no tranquillisers in those days, and therefore no way of restraining her while she was examined or given an injection. In the end, after she had been ill for weeks, it was decided that a doctor from Good Hope Hospital in Sutton should carry out blood tests to see if these would show up whatever complaint she was harbouring.

A doctor armed with morphine duly arrived and we wrestled to hold Sue still while he gave her an injection which should have calmed her down. Instead, it had the opposite effect and made her so excitable and hyperactive that by the time the doctor tried to take a blood sample Sue was racing round and round the cage while we looked on, helpless to stop her.

It was our first lesson in the unpredictability of tranquillisers in different species. After our nerve-wracking experience we learned that cats react in the same way as Sue to morphine, as do some humans. Sue never did have a blood test and continued to run a temperature for the next three months, with bouts of sickness followed by bouts of normality. Our hopes were constantly being raised that she was getting better, only to be dashed into despair when she became ill again. During the periods when she was in remission she would revert to her imperious demanding behaviour, and although we were terrified of losing her, sometimes I think we both had an unvoiced feeling that life would have been easier without having such a difficult animal on our hands; but there was no question that we loved her and that she returned our feelings.

When she was well enough we still took her to Sutton Park and it was on one of these visits that we discovered what was wrong. On this particular day Sue did something she had never done before: she flung herself at the grass and began to eat lumps of it until it made her violently sick. We were perplexed by her unusual behaviour, although we had seen it many times with our dogs, who have an inbuilt instinct to eat grass to make themselves sick when they have stomach upsets. Because of that knowledge we carefully examined the grass she had vomited and were amazed to find a long darning needle. We picked it up and looked at each other as it dawned simultaneously on both of us that this was the cause of Sue's problem. During one of her sewing sessions she must have swallowed the needle which had lodged in her stomach, setting up recurring infections.

Once her system had ridded itself of the offending needle, to our delight, Sue never looked back and made a complete recovery. Of course, she became an even bigger tyrant than before.

It was Nat who came up with the idea of finding Sue another chimp as a companion. 'It's obvious she is never going to be happy on her own, so why don't we get her a friend?' said Nat. 'Nothing can be worse than it is now and if it calms her down it will make life easier for all of us.'

It sounded logical and Sue's behaviour was so

intolerable that I was willing to try anything, so we set about locating a companion for our delinquent chimp. When we learned that a dealer in Manchester had just received a consignment of chimps we lost no time in going to see them. Others had beaten us to it, however, and we found to our dismay that the chimps we liked were already sold; the two we were offered were rejected immediately when one pulled my hair and the other gave me a vicious pinch.

'I am not having these,' I asserted. As I spoke I turned and found myself looking into the twinkling brown eyes of a small chimp.

'We'll have that one,' said Nat, echoing my thoughts.

It took a lot of haggling before the deal was struck and not before we had agreed to pay £300, a lot more than we had bargained for. Still, our new chimp's behaviour was very reassuring. She readily left her cage and clung to me until we were in the car, and she spent the whole of the journey back swinging happily from the sunblinds. We couldn't get home fast enough to introduce Sue to her new companion. On the way we decided to name our amiable newly acquired chimp Mickey, and fondly pictured Sue greeting her with open arms. We could not have been more wrong.

As soon as we let Sue out of her cage she leapt across the room and bit the intruder savagely on the arm. Mickey howled with pain and ran to us for protection, flinging her arms around us. From then on it was open warfare.

CHAPTER THREE

Outwitted by Chimps

That night we went to bed depressed and exhausted. Instead of solving Sue's problems we had doubled our own. The next day we had to confront our two protaganists and decide how to cope with their behaviour. We could only sympathise with Mickey, who had been the victim of an unprovoked attack, and blame ourselves for not effecting the introduction of the two chimps gradually or anticipating Sue's violent reaction to someone invading her territory. Too late to put back the clock, we had to put up with the consequences and devise some way of persuading them to live in harmony even if it was against Sue's wishes.

Sue had no intention of co-operating, however, and acted like the badly behaved spoilt brat that she was, shrieking and lunging at Mickey if she came near any of her toys. She guarded them jealously, fought over them, and stole any toy we had given to Mickey, landing her a hefty clout if she tried to retrieve it.

We took both of them daily to Sutton Park but had to keep them on long leads to stop Sue attacking Mickey or even turning on any unsuspecting child or adult who might come too near. And as the chimps could undo their collars we had to fit padlocks to them to prevent Sue from escaping and venting her wrath on poor Mickey.

They also had to be separated at bath-time or there would have been one almighty fight. When Sue realised that Mickey was waiting her turn she would linger over her ablutions as long as she could. She would splash around exuberantly, swamping the bathroom with foam and water until we tried to get her out, when she would steadfastly sit tight, refusing to move. We had to resort to bribing her with some titbit before she would relinquish her place in the bath.

Mickey, far more ladylike, quietly enjoyed her time in the soapy water, which inevitably was always cut short by Sue's bad behaviour. All this added an extra hour on to our already busy day and after we had shut the chimps safely in their cages for the night we would flop into armchairs totally worn out.

Both Mickey's life and ours were made intolerable and it caused many disagreements between Nat and myself. I constantly allowed them to get away with bad behaviour instead of chastising them, which quite rightly irritated Nat immensely until one day even I had come to the end of my tether. When Sue instigated yet another fight over a toy, I lost my temper and gave them both a clout on their ears. For an instant there was a shocked silence, followed by two screaming chimps throwing themselves into each other's arms and from that moment they were the best of friends.

They became inseparable, doing everything together – although Sue's superior intelligence always made her the leader. It had been fascinating to compare the two and from the beginning it was obvious that although Mickey was willing to please and always amiable, compared to Sue she was a total dunce. We spent hours trying to teach her skills which Sue had learned in minutes and Mickey would gaze at us with her big, trusting eyes and do it wrong time and time again. Quick-tempered, quixotic Sue was a quick learner while slow moving, slow-to-anger Mickey was a slow learner, but her loving nature made up for it and they both taught us such a lot.

We learned, for instance, how important it is to be scrupulously fair. Both Sue and Mickey would accept discipline if it was meted out justly, but if they were given a slap which they considered unfair they would make a fuss and refuse to have anything to do with us until we made our peace. They even accepted a smart nip from one of our cats or dogs when they were tormenting them and respected them for it.

It seems strange when now, fifty years later, it is considered unacceptable for human parents to chastise their children by giving them a light slap; they can even be prosecuted for doing so. Yet in primate and monkey societies slapping a youngster for unacceptable behaviour is the way they teach their offspring the difference between right and wrong and what is acceptable in their family groups. It keeps youngsters in line and gives them a guide as to how far they can go – which is important if one is going to keep them co-existing harmoniously in the group. When we talk about a breakdown of law and order in human society perhaps we should learn a lesson from our nearest cousins, who seem to have avoided problems in that direction.

Looking back I often wonder how we managed to keep running our business while adding to our collection of monkeys and keeping two demanding chimps happy. We would definitely have carried on in that fashion far longer if the chimps had not forced us to make a decision that would change our lives.

It happened one Sunday when Nat and I had closed the shop, taken the chimps for their walk in the park and then gone off for a well-earned lunch at a nearby hotel. It was the only time we had to ourselves when we could relax, and we lingered over our meal satisfied that all was well. Our feeling of well-being lasted during the journey home and we were laughing over one of the chimps' latest antics as we turned into Station Road – then stopped abruptly when we saw the crowd gathered outside our shop, their gaze turned upwards watching something in the flat windows.

We stared in horror as a cheer went up and a cushion flew out from the window, followed rapidly by newspapers, tins, clothes, dog pedigrees and lumps of coal.

Peering up, we were horrified to see Sue and Mickey looking down from the open window, enjoying all the attention and playing to the crowd by hurling everything they could lay their hands on down to the pavement below. A bag of sugar landed close to my feet and to my embarrassment I spotted a pair of my pink silk panties hanging from a nearby telephone wire.

We lost no time in pushing our way through the crowds and letting ourselves into the premises, to be greeted ecstatically by our delinquent chimps who were only too eager to show us what they had been doing, expecting the same approval from us as the heady applause they had received from their audience. We gazed around, taking in the devastation, not knowing whether to laugh or cry at the scene of utter destruction which assaulted our eyes. Having somehow managed to get out of their cages, the chimps had rampaged through the flat, opening the fridge and every store cupboard, emptying the contents of every container, jar or tin they could open.

The hallway was covered in treacle and coal, pillow feathers and jam trailed up the stairs, more treacle and coal coated the floor of the living room and even the bedroom had been invaded. Christmas presents that we had carefully wrapped and hidden under the bed had been opened by impatient hairy hands and thrown around. A large pink teddy bear that squeaked when moved lay surrounded by broken Pyrex dishes. We could only imagine that the noise he made had scared our pair of vandals and they had defended themselves from the strange pink creature by hurling the dishes at him.

Somehow we managed to keep calm and persuade our vandals back into their cages while we set about clearing up the mess, salvaging what we could from the wreckage. We forced ourselves to feed the chimps as usual and give them their baths before, tired out, they went to bed. We had not said much but we both knew that we just could not continue as we were. A drastic decision had to be made. From now on we had to be sensible and accept that our home was no longer suitable to house all of us.

It was the chimps who had brought us to this crossroads in our lives and we had the choice of going in two directions. We could get rid of Sue and Mickey so that we could continue to live in the flat and run our business, or we must find somewhere else more suitable where the chimps and ourselves could live in harmony. The decision was clearcut – a future without the chimps and the liabilities and responsibilities they brought with them, or we could keep them and face all the problems and difficulties, some of which we could anticipate and others that we could not even imagine.

We were exhausted but stayed up talking into the early hours of the morning until we came to a decision. In the end there was no choice to make. Neither of us could envisage life without our chimps or relinquishing our passionate interest in primates and monkeys.

Having established that we were both determined to continue our life with the chimps, we decided to start looking for a more suitable property the next morning.

When I finally went to bed the chimps were still fast asleep, oblivious to the fact that their future had now been decided. They had won the day. Outside, forgotten, my silk panties still fluttered triumphantly from the telephone wire as if proclaiming the chimps' victory.

When Nathalie's father was told about our decision he was delighted. He had always loved all our animals and now saw an opportunity to become more involved with them. Since Nat's mother's death six months previously he had been living alone down a secluded lane near the Staffordshire village of Hints. Just opposite, a parcel of land extending to three-quarters of an acre had come on the market and he suggested that we buy it and apply for planning permission to erect a bungalow built to our own design to accommodate us *and* the chimps. It was close enough to Sutton to enable us to commute to the shop every day and it would save Nat worrying about her father being on his own.

Buying the land was simple, finding an architect willing to design a house to our unusual specifications was not so easy. Our previous disastrous experiences of sharing every room with our chimps had left us with very firm ideas about what would allow us to preserve our sanity as well as living harmoniously with our two miscreants. We did not want to segregate them totally from us and lose the rapport and contact we had established with Mickey and Sue, but they did need to have some separate quarters of their own where they could play and have their own toys; somewhere which did not encroach upon our lives.

We decided that a special room should be built for the chimps, with barred windows and a steel door to separate them from the rest of the house, a room with central heating and a shelf running all around the walls where they could sit, climb and keep their toys. There would also be ropes and a climbing frame to keep them occupied. It also had to be secure enough to stop them escaping into the rest of the house to run riot and wreck the house and its contents. We would even insist on them having their own toilet installed. Nothing was too good for our chimps.

When they heard of our plan, people thought we were raving mad, as did the eminent architect friend of Nat's whom we approached. His reaction was one of horror at our suggestions and we got the distinct impression that he felt it would dent his reputation if anyone found out he was designing a bungalow for chimps. However, eventually he agreed to draw up some plans.

The location of the bungalow was perfect, tucked away down this quiet lane which meandered downhill away from a main road surrounded by forty acres of woods and fields which belonged to Nat's father, so although it was overlooked by passing traffic it was nicely secluded.

The profusion of trees near to the bungalow seemed the ideal place to provide Mickey and Sue with their favourite exercise, climbing and swinging from branches as they had done in Sutton Park.

We had become convinced that fresh air was an

extremely important ingredient in maintaining their health and well-being, and if we had to find a substitute for their outings in the park it would have to be somewhere contained and away from the public because of Sue's increasing aggression towards strangers.

The problem was solved when we spotted an advertisement for a lion cage which was for sale at a zoo near Bournemouth. Despite the high cost of transporting it, by the time we had fitted it with a roof it proved the ideal playground for our two chimps.

Taking stock of the progress we had made with our chimps we realised that our really big breakthrough had been in giving them access to grass and fresh air. We had learned that they had the same ability as ourselves to adapt to different climates as long as they had adequate heat in really cold or wet weather and so we planned something which met with almost unanimous disapproval from zoos, scientists and dealers: we installed grass runs for all our apes and monkeys.

'It is madness. They will pick up parasites from the grass and soil and they will die,' was the general consensus of opinion as they dismissed our theories, labelling us, as usual, as two batty women. Fortunately for our simian dependants, we ignored them and our animals continued to thrive in spite of the so-called experts' gloomy prophecies.

By the time we had installed the grass enclosures, planning permission for the bungalow was eventually granted. Work started on it almost immediately and although the workmen raised their eyes at the chimp room with its radiators and toilet they carried out the work speedily and thoroughly.

While we were waiting for it to be completed, an unforeseen incident happened which was to have a lasting and tragic effect on Sue. Nat was downstairs in the shop when a thunderstorm began. I heard the first growl of thunder in the distance which heralded a monumental thunderstorm. Terrifying bangs exploded overhead as torrential rain bounced off the pavement and jagged flashes of forked lightning lit the navy-blue sky.

One of the flashes of lightning seemed almost to come through the window and was followed by an ear-piercing shriek from the kitchen. When I rushed in from the living room I found Sue sitting on the stainless steel draining board with every hair on her head standing on end silhouetted against the window, her eyes wide and staring with shock.

It seemed that she had been struck by lightning, although within a few hours her hair returned to normal and she had apparently suffered no ill-effects. As she seemed to have made a full recovery we did not call the vet and it was only later that we would have cause to recall the incident.

Although the two chimps took up most of our time and interest we still continued to add other small monkeys to our collection. Some were on sale in the shop. Others became permanent residents and would accompany us when we moved to Hints.

For the time being all our energies and attention were concentrated on our new home.

Within six months it was finished and we moved ourselves in with the aid of Nat's brother and father. Little did our chimps know when they left the shop for the last time and jumped into the car expecting to go for their daily trip to Sutton Park that they were heading for pastures new. Introduced into their new home and familiar toys, they were quite happy to spend the next few hours exploring while we ferried the rest of our monkeys over in relays before arranging our own furniture.

Tired but satisfied that this was a new beginning with an exciting future, we fell into bed exhausted.

The next day we began our new routine, with Nat staying at the bungalow to supervise the care of our growing number of animals while I commuted to the shop to continue trading.

We felt secure and optimistic about the future. After all, by designing our own bungalow we felt that we had covered every contingency to make it safe and user-friendly for all its occupants. We were wrong. Within two weeks Mickey and Sue, despite all assurances from the builders that the chimps' room was extra secure, had ripped the radiators from the walls and we had no alternative but to let them back into our part of the house, which they thought was wonderful but drove us to distraction.

I sometimes wondered during the weeks that followed, if wrecking the radiators had not been part of some cleverly contrived plot to force us into co-habiting once more. To combat their insatiable energy and low threshold of boredom we reverted to taking Sue and Mickey into nearby fields and woods to tire them out so that we could have some peace.

The one concession we had made from the beginning was to allow the chimps to eat with us in the kitchen and we would share a companionable hour over dinner as we would with human friends.

The day the repairs to the chimps' room were completed we breathed a sigh of relief as Mickey and Sue were restored to their own territory. That summer, for the first time in years, we were able to entertain friends knowing the chimps were secure and happy in their own room. We congratulated ourselves on having found the ideal compromise for us all to live harmoniously.

However, we had not accounted for the cunning of our companions. Our self-satisfaction lasted all through summer and into winter – until we found ourselves outwitted by Sue, who made her move with all the skill of a chess-master.

We were in the kitchen and had just finished our evening meal when I made the fatal mistake of deciding to go to the coal-house to fetch a log for the fire in the lounge instead of taking the chimps straight back to their room. By the time I had reached the coal-house and was retrieving some logs I realised that Sue was beside me picking up a log herself. She carried it back into the house and I was so touched by her helpful gesture that I allowed her to put the log on the fire with me.

The next evening, as soon as she had finished her tea she scrambled off her chair and made for the coal-house, reappearing with a large log and stood by the lounge door with her eyes twinkling waiting for me to open it. I put paid to these antics by locking the coal-house door but Sue came up with another ploy to get into the lounge.

She would pick up empty milk bottles, grab my hand and pull me to the front door to open it so that she could deposit the bottles on the step before racing back to the lounge, where I would find her ensconced in her old place on the settee watching television. Even Nathalie, far more practical and sensible than I, gave in to the inevitable and Sue and Mickey were restored to their places in the lounge to watch unlimited television until bedtime.

Often unsociable to strangers, Sue did get on well with Renee Carley, our former postwoman who became the first member of our staff once we could afford her. Now that Renee, who was a heavy smoker, was spending more time with us, Sue became fascinated by this habit and watched carefully as Renee went through the process of taking a cigarette from a packet and lighting up. Feeling more confident, she would then put her hand out to ask to be given one herself. One day out of curiosity I asked Renee to give her a cigarette and light it for her.

Sue astonished us by taking the cigarette in her mouth, and lit it like a seasoned smoker. The next day she fetched a packet of cigarettes, offered one to Renee before taking one herself and then lit Renee's as well as her own with a match. She then sat watching television, tapping her ash into an ashtray without dropping any on to the floor and stubbing the cigarette out when it was finished.

It was a habit which we had to curtail but proved that, given the opportunity, a chimp as intelligent as Sue would soon pick up our human vices.

CHAPTER FOUR

Crossroads

Although there was only half an acre of ground surrounding the bungalow we decided that when any new type of monkey became available, we would add it to our collection. Every inch of space was utilised and Nat's father gave us tremendous support. He loved the animals and thought it was all great fun and happily spent his time helping to build more cages and runs for our growing collection. We put in neat walkways and a profusion of flowers between each cage and its grassy runs.

By now we had gained a reputation for being very knowledgeable in successfully rearing primates and monkeys, and ever more dealers beat a path to our door. One of these was Bob Jackson, who with his wife Margaret eventually opened Colwyn Bay Zoo. Bob had heard that we might be interested in another chimp and arrived on the doorstep with not one, but two: a funny little male called Bill whose wizened face wore a permanently perplexed expression and a fat, round-faced ugly female called Lucy whose looks belied her sweet nature.

Bob certainly used psychology on us that day when he suggested he leave both of them with us for the weekend so that we could make up our minds which one we wanted. Of course, we ended up with both.

We were constantly being offered more animals, often from people who had bought a monkey or chimp when it was tiny and cute and then found to their dismay that they could not cope with a mature animal.

People wrote to us from as far away as Africa, either for

advice or to beg us to take their unwanted monkey. One of these was a wealthy lady who lived in London and had started, like us, with a miniature zoo mainly stocked with Spider Monkeys, Marmosets and two chimps. Like most people, she managed to cope with her first chimp until he was five years old, when his behaviour began to change.

At her wit's end, she had him put down. We were horrified but afterwards acknowledged that having been a pet he would probably never have been able to be integrated into a group and that perhaps she had made the right decision. This woman kept in touch with us and years later when her other chimp, Mitzi, came into season, which heralded the beginning of unpredictable moods and behaviour, she asked us to take her in and we agreed. Although Mitzi eventually settled, she was always neurotic.

Acquaintanceship with another wealthy lady in Sheffield led to one of the most bizarre incidents in our increasingly colourful lives. She had bought a delightful baby chimp that she doted on, called Max. Spoiled and undisciplined, by the time Max was six years old he was totally unmanageable and dangerous and we refused to adopt him. Reluctantly she allowed him to go to Chester Zoo, but he would not settle and moped and went on hunger strike until they gave in and had to ask her to have him back.

Max never really recovered from this experience and continued to refuse food, barely eating, as we learned from the regular bulletins our friend would relay to us. One day we answered the door to find the distraught woman standing there in person. She could barely get her words out but kept waving in the direction of her Bentley which was parked in our drive. When we approached the limousine we could see a large figure sewn into a blanket lying on the back seat like a human body in a shroud. It was Max, who had died of malnutrition.

How his owner had managed to drive all the way from Sheffield down the A1 without some police patrolman spotting her macabre passenger I don't know. She had brought him to Hints so that he would be buried where there were other chimps. 'I know he will rest easier knowing he is amongst his own kind,' she told us tearfully.

To avoid offending anyone's sensitivities, Nat and I left it until dusk to begin digging an enormous burial hole away from any prying eyes. As we grasped the stiff body under its blanket shroud and staggered with it towards Max's last resting place, a sense of the ridiculous overcame us. It must have looked like a scene from a B horror movie and I wondered what other outlandish events would befall us because of our chimps.

We did not have to wait long to find out. Within days of Max's burial party we received a telephone call from our old friend Gerald Durrell, the famous naturalist and writer who had founded Jersey Zoo.

About to leave once more on one of his many expeditions, he was looking for someone to take care of his own chimp, Chumleigh, and felt that we would be ideal.

It seemed as though some kind of honour had been bestowed on us to be entrusted with the now famous Chumleigh, who had been immortalised in one of Gerald's best-selling books as well as appearing in films and television.

'You really are the only people I feel I can trust with Chumleigh,' Gerald said persuasively – forgetting to add until we had agreed that he was to be away for a year.

When he imparted this bit of information, warning bells began to ring – but how could we refuse such an eminent zoologist and friend?

Even so, I did stipulate that he must bring Chumleigh to spend the night with us to see if he would settle before we finally committed ourselves. Gerald thanked us profusely and he and his sister duly appeared with their celebrity chimp in the back of their car, clutching a wicker basket containing more toys than our chimps had seen in their lives. There were clothes, footballs, rubber rings, scooters, even a trampoline – all of which had been provided by the advertising company for which Chumleigh had been doing publicity.

Our very amenable chimp Vicky was playing in the garden when the trio arrived and when Gerald's sister pointed her out and asked her background I was happy to fill her in on Vicky's history.

When she had arrived as a young chimp she was suffering from pneumonia and had been very sick. For a week she was placed in an oxygen tent in our house until she recovered, which had caused her to bond with us and become a very loving, gentle chimp. When Gerald suggested that she might make an ideal companion for Chumleigh I readily agreed. I had bargained without Chumleigh, however.

The moment we tried to effect an introduction between the two chimps, Chumleigh turned his back on Vicky and snatched up his basket of toys and refused to let her near them. He hated her and our other chimps on sight. For all of his three years with Gerald he had been spoiled rotten, was used to being the centre of attention and getting his own way and had no intention of allowing our chimps anywhere near him.

When Gerald and I put him into one of our outdoor cages he was furious at such an indignity and screamed non-stop. Even when we went into the house for a well-needed cup of tea we could still hear him bellowing at the top of his voice just like a spoiled child.

Later that evening, when Gerry and his sister drove off to the hotel in Tamworth where they were spending the night, they were followed by Chumleigh's shrieks which echoed all the way up the drive and down the lane. The tantrum that he threw was so severe that he continued to scream throughout the evening, upsetting all our other animals. We were almost at the end of our tether when Gerald phoned at nine o'clock that night to see how he was settling in.

'He isn't,' I told him sharply. 'He's still at it, and if he doesn't stop you'll have to take him back with you.'

To combat the horrendous racket, Nat turned the sound up on the television to full blast to try to drown out the temper tantrum going on outside. We were so immersed in the programme that at first we did not realise that suddenly everything had gone silent. We turned the sound down and sure enough there were no more screams or bangs from outside.

'Thank goodness for that,' said Nathalie. 'He must have worn himself out at last.' And with that we retired to bed.

When Gerald rang early the following morning we told him that all was well and he set off home to Jersey. We ate a leisurely breakfast with still no sound from Chumleigh to disrupt the peace of the beautiful spring morning.

When we did go to see how he was faring we found ourselves staring at an extremely angry chimp whose mouth opened and closed constantly as if he was still screaming, but no sound came out. Chumleigh had not calmed down, he had simply lost his voice.

The twelve months he was with us seemed like an eternity, for Chumleigh was intractable and would neither mix with the other chimps or share anything with them. In fact, he is the only chimp in all my years of handling them who has ever really bitten me and meant it.

It was a relief when he departed back to Jersey and left us to concentrate on our growing collection.

We bought more animals from Bob Jackson, including a brown Woolly Monkey called McGamba, who looked just like a gorilla and wasn't at all tame, which in fact made him safer.

The tamer the monkey, the more potential it has to be dangerous, because monkeys are not afraid of people and when they become mature will sometimes attack the hands that feed them, whereas wild monkeys are always wary of the unknown and will choose to retreat from humans rather than have a confrontation. This applies to all wild animals. In the case of McGamba we had a mutual respect.

We had one gibbon called Lotus who enjoyed her freedom and rarely spent any time in her cage. She would sit on the roof of the bungalow surveying the surrounding countryside, but her main interest was in the activities of Nat's father's geese. She would watch as they settled on their nest to lay and then sneak down and, risking vicious pecks from angry beaks, would steal the eggs and clamber back to her place of safety on the roof to eat them.

Another of our acquisitions was a capybara, the largest living rodent; these animals resemble a scrubbing brush with no tail and long legs, and can grow to weigh 100 lb. Semi-aquatic, with webbed toes and a deposit of fat under the skin, these delightful creatures originate from the lakes and swamps north of the Parana River in Argentina and live on grasses and aquatic plants.

We christened our capybara Macginty and installed him in our small outdoor pool, where he would take advantage of being a semi-aquatic and go for a swim. Although he had his own outdoor quarters we would often find him curled up in the house drying on one of the beds.

In fact, every creature we had seemed determined to join us in the bungalow, from our Blue and Gold Macaw who would bang on the door to be let in, to the pair of baby Chinese Water Deer which we bought and bottle-fed. These beautiful fawns became so tame they were allowed to wander around the grounds and graze in the adjoining spinney, but when they tired of grazing they too would knock at the door and we would find them standing outside gazing at us with their doe-like eyes asking to be let in.

Nat and I also bought a pair of Kinkajous, or Honey Bears as they are sometimes known, although in fact they are members of the racoon family and live in the forests of South America. It was impossible not to fall in love with such beautiful nocturnal creatures. They are so cuddly with soft fur, sparkling eyes and a prehensile tail to enable them to climb. Their basic requirements are almost the same as monkeys, and so at first we had no problem with them.

The kinkajous slept in the room which housed the central-heating boiler, next to the chimps. They were quite happy there until one night we made the mistake of leaving a window open and they took the opportunity to embark on the first of many nocturnal adventures. The next morning when we found them missing we searched frantically around, only to discover them curled up in the coke hod by the outside boiler.

Deciding that they would not wander far, we deliberately left the window open after that so they could enjoy their freedom, and we would watch them in the deepening dusk of summer making gigantic leaps among the trees in the garden before returning at dawn to the coke boiler.

All through summer they followed the same routine until the mellow mists of autumn descended and they got the scent of the ripening apples in the orchard across the road. At six in the morning we were awoken by a telephone call from a neighbour to say that they had a pair of strange animals on the roof. We spent a morning up a ladder retrieving the hissing, spitting couple, who did not take kindly to being disturbed when they had settled down to sleep. After that incident we decided it would be prudent to keep them in, but no matter how hard we tried, our two kinkajous turned out to be a pair of Houdinis and in the end, reluctantly, we decided it would be safer for us and them if we sent them off to a zoo.

Nathalie and I were now totally absorbed with wild animals and had gained enormous experience and knowledge about their welfare. We were no longer considered a couple of eccentric women and zoo directors were treating us with respect.

The transition from having our private collection to becoming a commercial venture open to the public began in the same manner as the sequence of events which had brought us to Hints – more by accident than design.

Although we lived in a very secluded spot, our menagerie could be seen by the occupants of cars passing on the road which overlooked the property and it became a regular occurrence for people to arrive at the gate at weekends asking if they could see the animals. Some of them returned the following week bringing their friends; articles in the local papers created even more interest until every weekend in the summer the tiny lane was jammed with cars as we were invaded by families seeking admittance.

At first it was a novelty, but as the number of visitors increased it became a nuisance until it occurred to me that if, without any advertising or planning, we were inundated with people wanting to see exotic animals, we should not turn them away but should take advantage and make them pay. The income generated would help to keep our animals and finance improvements. Until then, all the running costs, including Renee Carley's wages, had been funded from our income from the pet shop. We had ploughed all our money into looking after our animals or adding new ones to our growing collection. Now we had an opportunity to make our hobby pay.

Like the events which initiated our move to Hints, it was a step that we had never planned or envisaged, just something which evolved as if we were being led in a certain direction for the future through our animals.

When Nat and I took the decision to open our private collection to the public and make a small charge, we knew that it would change our lives in some respects. But we had no idea that we were stepping on to a roller coaster which would result in us founding one of the most interesting and successful zoos in Europe.

Nor were we totally aware of the steep ups and downs that lay ahead when we embarked on what we innocently believed to be a simple move to help our limited finances and give our animals more security.

We applied for planning permission to open to the public and when Nat's father agreed that we should use one of his fields as a car park, permission was granted almost immediately.

One of the first items on the agenda was to hire more staff. We advertised locally for keepers and were fortunate to find ideal candidates in Dorothy Phillips and Jenny Minney, who made up the team with Renee Carley and ourselves.

Dorothy had not worked with exotic animals but with dogs and seemed to transfer that experience to strike up an immediate bond with our chimps, and all the animals seemed to sense Jenny Minney's devotion and rapport.

The other, most valuable member of our team was our vet, Mary Brancker. Many vets in that era were not prepared to consider treating anything other than domestic pets. In contrast, Mary was intensely interested by exotic animals and considered them a challenge. What she could not learn from veterinary books she would glean by contacting vets attached to major zoos and in that way became invaluable to us as well as becoming recognised as an authority in the zoological side of veterinary science.

It had not been our intention to create an all-female team but as our experience grew we found that women were more sensitive to animals' needs and moods than men and they were accepted more readily by our animals, who were used to being handled by women. Women also seemed to be more thorough than men in taking a pride in keeping cages and utensils clean.

Once our new staff had settled in and all felt capable of coping with the venture ahead, we opened to the public and to our delight became an instant success. In our wildest dreams we had not anticipated such a response when 400 people descended on us each weekend.

And we felt a sense of relief that the revenue they brought in more than justified the wages of the staff, the vet's bills and the innovations we were determined to make.

Both Nat and I had an enormous feeling of satisfaction when we saw the looks of wonder on the faces of the children who were seeing wild animals for the first time in their young lives. Or the sheer delight of parents who smilingly watched our macaw freely flying around in the trees or waited patiently by our newly built pool to watch the penguins being fed.

We were riding on the crest of a wave and it seemed that everything we touched had the sweet taste of success. We were blissfully ignorant that we would soon be facing bitter disaster and the heartache of losing two of those closest to us – Nat's father and our beloved chimp, Sue.

Nat's father had survived a heart attack before being struck down with cancer and sadly lost his fight against it.

Our grief at his loss was added to by the worry of Sue developing epilepsy, a condition that Mary Brancker believed had been triggered off two years previously when she had been struck by lightning. Starting with an occasional convulsion, Sue now began to have frequent fits, leaving her with an arm or a leg paralysed. She did eventually regain the use of her limbs, but as the seizures grew more severe she would be unconscious for longer periods and once became paralysed for some time from the waist down. Showing great devotion, Renee Carley would carry her round in spite of her weighing 100 lb.

Mary Brancker, too, would sit up at night with her and was always on call. Everyone who knew Sue loved her, and although we knew in our hearts it might be kinder to have her put down, we just could not face the idea. To us it was like giving a member of the family euthanasia – unthinkable. Until one night Sue had one of her fits and remained unconscious for so long that I rang Mary and told her that we felt that if Sue did not regain consciousness, the time had come to put her to sleep.

Mary had to drive nine miles to reach us, a journey which normally took half an hour. I kept looking at the clock, wondering why it was taking her so long and dreading the moment when she would arrive.

Later Mary told us that she had deliberately driven slowly, hoping against hope that Sue would have come round by the time she arrived. She hadn't, and we stood wordlessly by Sue's bedside as Mary gave her the lethal injection that would take her out of all her pain and suffering and out of our lives. Sue, our very first chimp, the one who had won our hearts, was only ten years old when she died and we have never forgotten her.

The sense of loss after Sue's death took its toll. When she was alive I don't think we recognised just how much we were living on our nerves; now we were left with empty depression.

If we were affected badly then Mickey suffered even more from losing her companion. For her it was worse because she did not understand why Sue was no longer there and she began to pine for her friend.

We were in a dilemma. We had no other chimps in Mickey's age group to whom we could introduce her, and after much heart searching we contacted Chester Zoo, who agreed to take her. We knew how upsetting it would be to part with her but it seemed the kindest option. At least Mickey would be with chimps her own age, and now she had reached maturity, she could be mated. Sadly, despite all the efforts to make her welcome and her introduction to eligible males, Mickey refused to settle down and died within a year.

Unbeknown to us, yet another tragedy lay ahead. We had four young chimps and had been given a baby, which had been hand-reared. When his owners gave him to us, they told us that they had been keeping him in a temperature of 80 degrees and advised us to do the same. Drawing on all our previous experience, we should have ignored their advice and followed our own instincts. Instead we complied with their request with no ill effects until a friend came to visit, bringing my godson who had a very bad cold.

His visit only lasted hours but it was long enough to pass the virus on to our young chimps, who became desperately ill, coughing and gasping for breath. On the vet's advice they were placed in oxygen tents: it was all we could do to help them.

The baby died within twelve hours and within days we

had lost three others. Only one, Vicky, survived. Nothing of that enormity had befallen us before and we were shocked and depressed. It seemed that, suddenly, everything was falling apart.

The only thing we were thankful for were the continuing queues of people who arrived every weekend to see the animals. Without their support we would have been in dire straits. Unfortunately, even they brought us more problems.

Nat's brother had inherited their father's house and had moved in with his wife, planning to lead a peaceful country life. However, their dream became a nightmare every weekend when the quiet country lane turned into a busy thoroughfare, with cars queuing to get into the car park which was right beside their house, many overflowing and resorting to parking directly in front of their home. Their privacy was also invaded when people peered over the hedge and looked into their window. It did not help that neither he nor his wife were enamoured of our collection, disapproved of the zoo and thought we were mad to have started one.

They constantly complained about the loud whooping of our gibbons and the piercing chatter of the chimps. Relations between us were extremely strained, but there was no way that we could contemplate closing the zoo. Only by being open to the public could we afford to keep our animals and we had no intention of parting with them.

If it had not been for our Nilgai, a large antelope who came from the Indian peninsula, we might have been able to keep an uneasy truce, but his antics were the straw that broke the camel's back.

In the wild, the surefooted Nilgais would travel through mountainous terrain, making spectacular leaps from rock to rock, across streams and ditches and other obstacles. Our Nilgai was no exception and on that fateful day had escaped into the orchard and from there made a bid for freedom, producing a leap of such magnitude that it not only cleared our fence but the lane and Nat's brother's fence. Unfortunately it landed right in front of Nat's sister-in-law, who threw up her hands to bar its way. Turning neatly on its hocks, without hesitation the Nilgai leapt back across the road into our orchard.

Minutes later, Nat's brother arrived and told us that this time we had gone too far and he wasn't prepared to let matters rest. We had heard these threats before and did not take them seriously. Besides, what could he do?

That afternoon we found out. He was no longer allowing us to use his field as a car park. Without it there was no way we could continue in business. The sheer volume of cars at the weekend would block the road and all the neighbours would be up in arms. Any complaints to the local council and they would inevitably step in and close us.

Once more we were faced with the same two choices – to do the unthinkable and give up our animals, or to find another location – not only to relocate them but to open a full-scale zoo.

CHAPTER FIVE

Twycross – The New Challenge

Once we had made the decision there was no looking back. Any feelings of depression that had lingered after the catalogue of disasters that had befallen us were left behind as we planned a new start and a brighter future. We already had enough animals to form the nucleus of a full-scale zoo and the backing of an enthusiastic public to keep the money rolling in; all we had to do was find the right premises and the money to buy it.

We were determined to stay in the Midlands, where we were already known to the public and where we had such reliable staff. We canvassed local estate agents but soon discovered that finding the dream place we had envisaged was not going to be easy.

One of the properties we went to view was Norton Grange, near the village of Twycross in Leicestershire; an imposing, sixteen-roomed Victorian residence, it was a former vicarage and latterly the home of Master of the local Hunt, Kenneth Beeston, who had kept his horses in the row of stables behind the house, where there was also a range of brick outbuildings.

Set in twelve acres of countryside, on paper it sounded ideal, but when we saw it we were filled with dismay. The house groaned at the fate that had befallen it over the years. The beautiful oak staircase had been painted yellow, likewise the oak panelled doors. There was no central heating and the paper was hanging off the walls with mould and damp. Giant fungi clung on to the cellar beams reminiscent of *Quatermass*-like creeping slime, and the so-called tack room boasted red walls with a black ceiling.

It was an eyesore, totally unsuitable except for the outbuildings, and would cost a fortune to heat and to restore it to its former glory. We crossed it off our list and set about viewing other properties, but nothing that was in our limited price range fitted the bill and we kept returning to Norton Grange, which drew us like a magnet despite all its faults.

By now winter was approaching and we needed to make a decision. Taking the bull by the horns we put in an offer for the property and found that apart from ourselves the only other interested party was the local authority, who wanted to open it as a remand centre.

Deciding to take the plunge, we applied to Market Bosworth Council for planning permission to open a zoo and three months later it was granted. They probably thought that a zoo was preferable to a home for delinquents – just! Since making that first decision to allow a zoo and recognising the potential it had for bringing employment into the area, the Council have given us continuing support and have been tremendously enthusiastic about our conservation and wildlife educational programmes for young people.

If we were thrilled by their positive attitude, our bank manager was not. When we approached him with our plan to buy the property and detailed our zoo project, he refused to advance us the £12,000 to buy the property plus a further £13,000 to convert buildings, renovate the house and build new quarters for our animals.

Although we had collateral in the bungalow at Hints, which we eventually sold for £9,000, and Nat had some securities, the bank manager considered it an extremely dubious venture and kept us waiting for his decision. In the end I lost my temper and told him, 'If you don't back us we will close our account and take our business to the bank over the road.'

My threat, which was sheer bravado, had the desired

effect. He did not like it but he grudgingly agreed to the loan.

We moved into Twycross in 1962 – during one of the severest winters in history. Heavy snowfalls covered the frozen landscape, giving Norton Grange the grim appearance of a Victorian workhouse. There was no heating inside the house except for our tiny electric fires which made no inroads into the cold, clammy atmosphere where plaster and wallpaper hung from the walls and fungus sprouted in the cellar. Nat's brother, who had been the catalyst of our move, took one look at the sorry state of our new home and said, 'If you don't have central heating installed you won't survive the winter.'

'How do you think we can afford it?' Nathalie demanded, but he merely repeated his warning before departing to his own cosy, centrally-heated home.

We looked at each other speechlessly and set about making the house, or at least one or two rooms, habitable. No matter what setbacks or inclement weather, we had to stick to our schedule to open our zoo to the public at Whitsun, the deadline by which time we calculated our money would have run out. We still had to pay Renee, Dorothy and Jenny, our three intrepid members of staff who were holding the fort, looking after the animals at Hints until we were ready to move them to Twycross.

Without the help of my brother, who was out of work at the time, and an old friend of ours, Geoff Ingram, we would never have been able to achieve our goal. The two men worked in impossible conditions, braving the extreme elements that lingered through February and March when the ground was so hard that they could not get a spade into it. They had to resort to working indoors to weld the bars of cages.

Progress was slow and it soon became clear that if we were to open on time we would have to take on more labour. We hired a private firm to erect the chimps' outdoor runs while Geoff and my brother concentrated on converting the inside of the brick cowshed into heated indoor quarters for the chimps. We all worked like Trojans as the minutes ticked inexorably by towards the dreaded deadline.

We cleared undergrowth to make a drive leading into the zoo from the main A444. The barren twelve-acre fields were prepared so that the ready-made buildings we had ordered could be erected and pathways laid between them. Easter arrived and we were still desperately behind with our plans.

In the end we put an advertisement in the local paper for odd-job men and the fifty applicants who turned up certainly fitted the description. Many of them were distinctly odd but were glad of the chance to earn some money. We set our motley, unskilled crew to work digging pools for the flamingos and penguins, laying turf and paths, putting up fences, and transforming the barren waste into an interesting, attractive landscape for our animals and their visitors. By the end of May most of our tools had disappeared and so had our labourers, but we now faced the forthcoming Opening Day with more confidence.

The stable block had become the chimps' quarters, the garage was destined to be the Tea Bar and the old free-range poultry house was turned into a Pets' Corner; toilets were installed for the public. One part of the field had been designated as a picnic field especially with school parties in mind.

Our activities had caused a great deal of local interest and we were interviewed by local radio, newspapers and television, which gave us invaluable publicity for the big day. We even managed to persuade television celebrity Jean Morton, who at that time presented ATV's children's programme *Tingha and Tucker*, to perform the official opening.

By now paintbrushes were out as the remaining band of workers put the finishing touches to pens and buildings. Then Nat and I and our three trusty female keepers tackled the last-minute task of moving the fifty animals from Hints to have them installed in their new quarters ready for the opening.

What a house move it proved to be. Some of the inhabitants at Hints did not take kindly to being uprooted; one or two of the smaller monkeys decided to escape and had to be recaptured by our harassed keepers.

It took a whole afternoon to round up the Nilgai and the Chinese Water Deer, who had been living in the spinney and took a dim view of changing their habitat. They ran backwards and forwards through the bushes, leaving us panting breathlessly after them. This stampede through the woods from one end to the other went on for hours until we eventually managed to drive them into a makeshift pen and then into the horsebox. By the time they set off for Twycross it was dusk and we were all exhausted.

The one creature left behind was the wallaby, which effortlessly bounded away leaving us standing, and we had no alternative but to leave him for another day. We saw him gazing after us as we drove away, a solitary silhouette against the horizon. Two days later we managed to recapture him.

Easier to move were our six flamingos and the penguins, who marched dutifully into their waiting crates which were placed in the back of our van, filling the vehicle with an overwhelming smell of fish. We only had one escapee, a macaw who fled into one of the trees at Twycross. He walked in through the front door of Norton Grange two days later, giving it his seal of approval.

I left the chimps, all five of them, until the morning of our Opening Day because I knew they would be easy to move. I led Rosie and Sam and the rest by the hand into their travelling boxes and headed back to the zoo for the opening ceremony. I had not bargained for the queues of cars which were already forming as I approached the zoo, getting caught in a minor traffic jam before managing to drive through before the real crush began.

When we saw the number of vehicles lined up waiting to get into Twycross we could hardly believe it; thousands of people, taking advantage of a warm sunny day, had turned out and the road was packed with cars in a traffic jam which stretched back for miles.

Our delight at this large turn-out turned to panic when our visiting celebrity failed to make an appearance and the stage we had erected for our star guest stood empty. Noon came and went. By now we were getting more agitated and so were the crowds.

Playing for time while Nat went to find out what had happened, I took Rosie on to the stage and went through some of her tricks, which pacified the crowd for a time until they became even more restive and catcalls came from the audience.

'This is a con. We came to see a celebrity,' one angry woman shouted.

'You got us here under false pretences,' shouted another.

At this point, Nathalie stepped in to inform them that she had spoken to the television company and that Jean Morton was on her way. She eventually turned up two hours late, looking totally harassed. She had been stuck in the same traffic jam as everyone else who was coming to the zoo. Her arrival calmed the impatient audience, thank goodness, and after doing a little show with the television puppets, she declared the zoo officially open.

We breathed a sigh of relief but our headaches were far from over. By the end of the day we realised that, despite all our careful planning, we had not taken into account the sheer volume of people who were coming through the gates. We had innocently believed that running a zoo would be the same as our small collection at Hints only on a bigger scale, and we had totally underestimated the demand for car parks, tea and toilets.

That first day highlighted all the flaws in our plans. We had expected at the most fifty or sixty cars and had made just one opening which served both as entrance and exit, creating a complete bottleneck. It was chaotic and got worse as, during the first month, we attracted 2,000 visitors a week.

Our tiny Tea Bar had long queues and so did the toilets. If that was bad enough, it was even worse when neither of them functioned. That first month brought home to us that if we were to cope with the coming Bank Holiday crowds we had to build more toilets and a larger café.

When we first took over the property it was surrounded by farms, and in those days nearly all of them were dairy farms with herds of cows which had to be milked. At milking time the milk had to be cooled, which required vast quantities of water which affected the water supply to the zoo so that the pressure was either very low or non-existent.

The water supply was also controlled by pumps at a nearby town and occasionally one or both of these would cut out, resulting in no water for the toilets or for the busy tea urns. It did not take a genius to work out that where there was tea you must have toilets that flush.

We learned this the hard way when one of the girls from the café came running over to tell us that there was no water for the tea urns and that the toilets would not flush. We rang the emergency water service only to be told that at this time of day the farmers were milking and using more water to cool the milk, and since we were only served by a small water main the pressure fell and our supply would become a mere trickle for a while.

As I headed for the café to explain matters to waiting customers, our Prairie Marmots saved the day. A distraught woman rushed out of one of the toilets shouting, 'There's a strange animal in the loo!'

A crowd gathered as I changed course and ran over to the toilets. There, sitting on his haunches in the corner of one cubicle looking surprised at all the fuss was one of our buck-toothed Prairie Marmots, also known as Prairie Dogs, a perfectly harmless creature from South America but enough to give some unsuspecting lady a fright when she found herself locked in the loo with one.

A cheer went up from the crowds as I fetched a carrying box and retrieved him, only to find when I arrived back at his enclosure that our whole group of Prairie Marmots had decided to demonstrate their ability to burrow underground for long distances by tunnelling out. Sightings of epidemic proportions kept the crowds entertained for the whole afternoon as one emerged near the ice cream kiosk and another appeared in the rose beds.

Our gardener, who had lovingly planted the borders with flowers and shrubs, reported that strange gaping holes had appeared beside nearly every plant. He was completely mystified until he spotted a cheeky buck-toothed face smiling at him from one of the tunnels. Ordinarily, the marmots' escapades would have been annoying, but that day we could only be thankful that they had created a distraction which helped visitors forget the non-flushing toilets and the urns suffering from drought.

For weeks afterwards we kept retrieving the marmots from various parts of the zoo, even from a local farm whose puzzled owner had telephoned to say they had spotted a strange animal digging a large hole in the middle of their wheatfield. Nat and I arrived to find one of our missing marmots happily tunnelling downwards as if heading for Australia. We caught him easily but were thankful that it was summer, otherwise he could have hibernated and we would never have found him. We made sure that this Grand Escape never recurred by increasing the width of the dry moat in the marmots' enclosure and by covering it with concrete. That was one problem solved! But now we had even more important matters to attend to if our new zoo was to survive.

Twycross Zoo was not connected to mains sewerage, which proved extremely problematic. It was always on a busy day or a Bank Holiday when the crowds were queuing to use the loos that a serious blockage occurred. How do you explain to your visitors that there is no tea and no toilets either?

Our electrical supply was also temperamental. As houses for the primates were added with underfloor central heating, the power supply had a nasty habit of blowing a fuse just as the oven and chip-fryer in the cafeteria were switched on. They say you learn by experience and we learned the hard way, running the gauntlet of angry visitors who had queued on a hot day only to be told when they arrived at the counter that there was no water or electricity to make the tea.

'Call this a café!' was one of the more polite jibes hurled at us.

Nat and I realised that before we were swamped with August Bank Holiday crowds, it was absolutely imperative that we not only build another café and more toilets, but that we install new water mains, a substation, drainpipes and fat traps, all of which were enormously costly. Somehow we had to find the money to do all this or face going out of business so, once more, we increased our overdraft.

It was a pattern we came to recognise over the years as the zoo grew bigger; more crises would arise, creating the need for more buildings and equipment. To this day we have carried out at least one major new construction every year, ploughing all our hard-earned profits back into the zoo to make it more attractive to our visitors as our facilities improved and developed.

Although initially we knew nothing about catering, our instincts told us not to let a catering company take over that side of the business because if the food was not up to standard the zoo would be blamed, not the company.

It was Nat's brother who took that problem off our hands by offering to take charge of the whole catering operation for the first year, from engaging the staff to managing the cafés. He said afterwards that supervising an all-female staff was an experience he would not wish to repeat: it was the worst twelve months of his life!

We started out offering tea, sandwiches and cakes, but as demand grew so did our menu. The next addition by popular request was fish and chips, when it was not unusual at Bank Holiday times to run out of chips because the delivery van was stuck in a queue of cars.

Over forty years tastes have changed. Burgers and buns are now in great demand as well as lasagne, curry, chilli con carne and jacket potatoes with various fillings, but the basics that we served in the beginning – teas, sandwiches, cakes and ice-cream – are still the all-time favourites.

Now we are certainly better organised, the facilities are vastly improved, and management excellent and more than qualified to deal with emergencies which thankfully crop up less frequently.

Today the staff have to qualify by gaining a certificate in hygiene, which includes learning how to take the temperature of pies and ice cream throughout the day and record it on a chart. Their outdoor clothes have to be left in a room offset to the cafeteria where they are required to don overalls and hats before commencing cooking operations. Hands must be washed in a separate basin to where food like lettuce and vegetables take their ablutions. Germs are a nasty word and flies are even worse. Today each employee has a designated job complete with job description. In the old days we had to be jack-of-all-trades and work all hours. No one had time to fall out; we were too tired to disagree.

After our first year we found that we had attracted 80,000 visitors through the gates and needed still more facilities. Once more we had to borrow money to allow us to build another café for the following spring, which meant that we would have two cafés with a joint seating capacity of 500 – a far cry from when we sold teas and ice cream on the terrace at Hints.

A temporary building was erected to act as a gift shop from which we sold postcards, key rings, souvenirs, books and cuddly toys, which brought in more revenue to help with the high running costs which escalated during winter.

Another vital improvement was to make separate entrances and exits so that the traffic flowed more easily. We were lucky enough to have the opportunity to buy a further fifteen acres of land adjoining the zoo which was largely swallowed up by being converted into another car park as our weekend trade had grown to over 1,000 cars.

Many of the car-parking areas today are mown grassland, which is ideal if you want to picnic beside your car; this has become a big attraction at the zoo. But if it is wet and we get torrential rain it can be a nightmare on busy days. It just turns into mud, glorious mud, so that on occasions visitors' cars have to be towed off with a tractor. Most visitors will accept this with a smile, but just occasionally we have had an owner with a rather posh Daimler or Mercedes who does not appreciate seeing his precious limousine spattered with mud and will storm into the office to demand ten pounds to take it to the car wash.

At the other end of the scale there are the teenagers with their first car whose idea of getting it out of the mud is to jam their foot down on the accelerator so that its wheels churn up the ground and they dig themselves deeper into the mire. We have dug out quite a lot of these while the crestfallen owner looks on. Trying to explain that if he had been lighter on the accelerator, the car would have moved, is usually met with an unprintable retort.

Over the first few years, most of our capital was taken up by purchasing more land, until today the area of the zoo is now 60 acres. The land became available as farms in the vicinity changed over from dairy to arable, partly due to an outbreak of foot and mouth disease in 1967 when hundreds of cattle had to be slaughtered and thousands of acres of farmland came under strict quarantine restrictions.

It was a worrying time for us, too, as the outbreak of the disease crept nearer to Twycross and at one point we were on the verge of making a decision to close the zoo to the public until the Ministry of Agriculture could give the all-clear. All our animals had to be kept under close observation; particularly the paddock animals like goats, camels, deer and llamas. We took very strict precautions. A barrier of disinfectant was put at the main entrance and similar barriers were laid down outside all the enclosures with strict instructions that all staff must scrub their boots with disinfectant to prevent any infection being carried inside. Our stock of animals was irreplaceable and it would have been a terrible tragedy if the disease had struck any of them.

The Ministry gave out warnings for people to keep off farmland. Rambling associations were asked to restrict their members to the highways, and anglers were told to stay at home until the crisis was over. We were lucky. The zoo could have been closed for an indefinite period with disastrous effects on our finances, but fortunately the epidemic abated with none of our animals being affected and in the end the scare resulted in doing us a good turn.

Many of the farmers who had been badly hit decided to change over to arable farming; some also wanted to sell parcels of land adjoining the zoo, which was very much to our advantage.

As well as providing more car parking, the area that was once open grassland is now an attractive landscape filled with hundreds of bushes, deciduous trees and conifers. The appearance of Twycross Zoo is far removed from the old vicarage with its garden and small greenhouse. The interior of the former Norton Grange has also changed and been restored to its former glory. The gaudy paint has long since been removed, the oak doors and oak staircase stripped to reveal the seasoned grain of natural wood and we have the ultimate luxury. Central heating.

CHAPTER SIX

Lounge Lizards and Other Creepy Crawlies

It was winter but a blast of heat met me as I opened the lounge door and a rancid, pungent odour assailed my nostrils. I wrinkled my nose with distaste and caught a glimpse of a pale, bland, yellow eye staring at me across the room from a glass case as the snake slowly uncoiled itself.

Our lounge, the best room in the house, looked like The Chamber of Horrors. Furniture was crowded into the middle of the room, and was surrounded by boxes and vivaria containing the most undesirable guests we had ever entertained. Peering out from their temporary accommodation were pythons, boas, large snakes, small snakes, lizards, spiders, toads, tree frogs and two eighteen-inch long Giant Iguanas whose tongues flicked in and out as they watched me enter the room.

Gazing into one of the glass cases I could see the red furry knees of a Tarantula lurking in a corner. Next to him in another glass tank, the red hairy legs of a Chilean Rose Spider waving at me. I was always aware of their presence and they never failed to give me the creeps.

Before I stepped inside, I looked around warily at the radiators and at the rug in front of the fireplace. I had already had two shocks, one when I had found a six-foot python curled up behind a radiator, and the next when I almost trod on a small lizard, which had escaped and taken refuge under the rug. The only comforting thought was that at least none of these creatures was poisonous.

For two months now, Nat and I had been forced to co-habit with reptiles and I blamed it all on little boys. Had it not been for them and their constant demands to see snakes and creepy crawlies, we would never have embarked on building a Reptile House and buying the creatures to fill it. I couldn't wait for the building to be finished so that we could rid ourselves of our unwanted lodgers and return to normality.

Neither Nat nor I would ever have exhibited reptiles from choice, but the fascination they held for children – especially small boys – could not be ignored. Time and again we heard the vociferous cry, 'Where are the snakes?'

Mums and Dads clamoured to see lions and tigers, birds of prey or paddock animals, but it seemed that snakes and reptiles were top of the list for their offspring. At first we tried to satisfy them by providing two large glass vivaria, one containing a boa constrictor, the other a baby alligator called Harold, but they wanted more and in the end, despite our limited capital, we had to bow to public demand and erect a proper Reptile House. It seemed ironic that our first major construction at the zoo should be for creatures in which we ourselves had very little interest.

Nat and I had no knowledge of snakes or reptiles, the kind of housing they needed or the temperatures in which they should be kept. In the end we sought the help of Ray Legge from Belle Vue Zoo, an expert in snakes and reptiles who had designed several Reptile Houses. Having no suggestions of our own to make about the design of the House, as our knowledge was too limited, we gave Ray a free hand. The only thing I insisted upon was that we would not have any poisonous snakes or reptiles in our collection, since they would be a hazard to keepers and the public.

Ray did us proud. He designed a stunning modern building with a central display of glass cases in which to house our snakes and lizards so that visitors could be afforded maximum viewing as they walked round the aisle. The walkway stretched around the building and brought the visitors back to where they had started, at the sunken pool where Harold the alligator, who had now grown to a massive six feet, and his equally impressive companion lay basking in shallow heated water, their eyes staring unblinkingly at their awed audience.

While Ray got busy we visited dealers to search out the more attractive-looking reptiles, lizards and spiders for our collection, placing our orders and paying for them as we went along, giving our suppliers the date of completion of the House as their delivery date. The Reptile House was to be built during our slackest period, just after Christmas, and was scheduled to take six months to complete, which coincided with the time it would take us to gather together our collection of exhibits.

We ordered bright green tree frogs which have adhesive discs on the tip of each finger and toe for clinging to vertical surfaces; tree pythons from Papua that curl up in the branches of trees where their colouring acts as a camouflage among the brilliant green jungle vegetation; Rainbow Boas from South America, the largest and most elaborately marked lizards from the lowlands of Mexico and South America, and bottle-green Water Dragons. The only poisonous specimens among them were the pink and black Gila Monsters from Arizona.

For insect lovers we included large tropical leaf insects with flattened bodies and wings that expand in such a way that they resemble the faded shade of a brown leaf. It was a colourful and interesting collection, which we hoped would appeal to everyone, but we had never anticipated them taking up residence in our lounge.

And yet we should have known from bitter experience that when the builders estimated that the Reptile House would take six months to complete, some problems would crop up to prevent it being finished on time. Like all our winter-time developments, we should have been prepared for the inevitable bad weather conditions that would prevail to prevent the construction meeting its deadline.

'It's no good – the weather is too bad and there is a shortage of materials,' declared the foreman in the face of our protests.

Nat and I looked at each other as the full enormity of his announcement hit us. The reptiles were ordered, paid for and due to be delivered any day. We spent the next few frantic hours ringing around the dealers pleading with them to delay deliveries, but our pleas fell on deaf ears. They did not want to keep our snakes and lizards any longer and insisted we took them.

The first delivery van arrived before we had time to organise any alternative accommodation for the occupants of the two boxes they left with us; one contained two curled-up six-feet-long Reticulated Pythons, the other two very lively Giant Iguanas, at least eighteen inches long.

Tropical snakes and lizards have to be kept in a temperature of at least 80 degrees Fahrenheit and none of the zoo buildings had that kind of intense heating. The only possible place we could keep them was in the house, and the only room which had enough radiators to sustain the correct temperature was our lounge – and so it was that our undesirable visitors were installed.

The smell they gave off after they were fed was totally repugnant. We had to have a special lock put on the door to keep out unsuspecting visitors, for the shock of walking into the room could have given them a heart attack. Of course, there was the odd occasion when our slithering snakes had their uses. If any unwanted visitors turned up or outstayed their welcome, offering to show them into the lounge invariably made them beat a hasty retreat.

No one was more relieved than I was when the Reptile House was finally completed and our scaly guests could be transferred to their new home where, I am delighted to report, they successfully fulfill their role in making little boys happy.

By now it had dawned on us that we could no longer only buy animals which were of interest to us; we had to provide a wider range of animals that fitted the expectations of our visitors. Our intentions had always been to collect the rarer primates and try to breed from them, but in those days our attitude was quite unusual. Years ago, most zoos simply provided a whole variety of animals on exhibition to attract the public, with no thought of conservation. Today, zoos tend to specialise in one species and the public is sophisticated and educated enough to appreciate what they are doing.

Left to ourselves, Nat and I would have carried on buying animals of our own choosing, continuing to concentrate on extending our collection of primates and monkeys. Now we realised we had to bow to public opinion. Time and again walking round the zoo we would overhear loud comments like, 'Where are the lions and tigers then?' Or, 'This place is boring. They've only got monkeys.'

Bearing these comments in mind, we decided to look around for some tigers. Compared to apes and monkeys, their needs were fairly simple – a large, suitably secure landscaped run and a small cosy den for shelter and sleeping quarters. We found just what we were looking for when we saw two hand-reared tiger cubs, a male called Sultan and a female named Suki, advertised in a magazine. We went to see them and they seemed healthy and full of fun and games, the ideal pair to fit in with our philosophy of always buying baby animals.

The tiger cubs were brother and sister and would have mated when they reached maturity. Before then we hoped to have added another tigress to our collection to prevent inbreeding. At that time far less thought was given to future breeding than in present times. Today the breeding of animals is much more scientifically controlled and inbreeding is avoided whenever possible.

Tragedy followed. We were appalled and disillusioned when within a week, our female cub began having fits and, despite veterinary treatment, died. We were now left with a male cub with no mate, which presented us with a very real problem. Unless we found a female cub to integrate with our fine male as soon as possible, their liaison was fraught with danger; unless a male tiger bonds with a female it can become aggressive and attack a newcomer.

After much searching we finally located a female cub of the right age in Holland. Buying Begum was simple; arranging for her to come to England now that the new quarantine laws were more stringent, presented us with more of a problem.

Firstly, we had to build our own quarantine quarters and have them approved and licensed. When we had fulfilled all the criteria we then had another setback. We discovered that the rules and regulations stipulated that our tigress was not allowed to share a cage with our male during her time in quarantine, which defeated the object of the exercise.

We overcame the problem by shipping our male tiger cub to Holland overnight so that he could be introduced to his new mate and they could then travel back to England and go into our quarantine quarters together. It was a waste of time and money, but the only solution.

They made a perfect pair and when they were two years old, the female tiger gave birth to her first litter, four tiny striped cubs with closed eyes who mewed and purred like kittens. Our delight was short-lived, however, for after a few days we noticed that some of the cubs were not feeding. Only then did we discover that the tigress had two malfunctioning teats and could not cope with feeding all four cubs.

Again it was our stalwart Renee Carley who volunteered to hand-rear three of the cubs, leaving the mother to cope with just one. Every night we could hear the sound of plaintive mewing from Renee's bedroom as the cubs demanded to be fed. They stayed in her room until they were three months old and could feed themselves.

After this experience we decided that if we were to breed tigers it might be sensible to buy another female tiger who would not have a problem rearing cubs, even if she did have trouble integrating with our male. In fact, our new tigress never did bond with him and would spit and snarl at him except when she was in season, when she would allow him to mate with her. In the end we had to segregate her and build her another house. Over the years, our tiger-breeding programme at Twycross has turned out to be a great success, and I am proud to say that our progeny have been sent all over the world to found breeding pairs in other zoos.

Shortly after we acquired the tigers we also bought two hand-reared lion cubs; very attractive, gentle animals, but when they matured they never mated. At a time when lion cubs were fetching high prices ours remained celibate. The bottom dropped out of the market for lion cubs with the innovation of safari parks, where greater numbers of lions were allowed to breed prolifically and we were thankful then that ours had not added to the lion population. Safari parks and zoos became so overpopulated, in fact, that lion cubs were just kept until they were older and no longer so cute – then they were put down.

When, years later, our lioness died from old age, leaving us with a lonely old lion on our hands, I could not bear to see him moping about on his own. A local zoo was closing down and their two lionesses were to be put to sleep; we intervened and bought them as companions for our lonely lion. We need not have bothered, for within three months the poor old chap was dead and we were now left with two lionesses. Again the public forced our hand by constantly asking where was our lion. We had no intention of breeding so how could we take in another male?

The solution came when we attended a zoo conference and the director of Belfast Zoo happened to mention that he had a marvellous lion which had just had a vasectomy. This operation was preferable to neutering, which has the side effects of causing the lion to lose his growth of mane and look moth-eaten, and to kill his interest in sex stone dead.

In contrast, a vasectomised lion retains his interest in

sex, grows a magnificent mane and has a glowing coat. I jumped at the chance of acquiring him. 'We'll call him Parkinson,' I told Nat, which seemed appropriate as TV presenter Michael Parkinson had just announced that he had undergone a vasectomy. Parkinson duly arrived and took up residence with our lionesses, satisfying them, our visitors and ourselves, as we did not have to worry about endless litters of unwanted lion cubs.

Again bowing to public demand, we had turned the old poultry house into a Pets' Corner with more domesticated and cute animals which children love to see. Rabbits are one of the favourite animals and we have various types to add more interest, including Dutch, French and Dwarf Lops, who look very attractive with their long floppy ears. And although many of the children have hamsters as pets at home they still cluster around to watch our Syrian Hamsters collecting their food in their pouches; and other assorted hamsters playing and grooming each other.

We also have Cameroon Sheep; small, very pretty, brown-coloured ewes that produce very appealing lambs every spring. These are always popular with visiting children and their families.

The most popular creatures in our Pets' Corner at Twycross have to be the Vietnamese Pot-Bellied Pigs, with their short legs, pot bellies, black bodies and slit eyes. Because they breed so prolifically and their piglets are so incredibly cute, they have sparked off a craze for people wanting to have them as pets. As the sows produce litters of up to ten or twelve piglets which can sell for ridiculously cheap prices, breeders have cashed in by indiscriminately breeding from them and flooding the market.

This process has created a lot of profit for breeders and a lot of suffering for the pigs. For as the cute piglets grow into large, mature pigs, owners suddenly find themselves confronted with the problem of having a fully grown pig in their small back garden or even in the house. In consequence, many animal rescue centres are inundated with calls from desperate owners wanting to get rid of their cumbersome pets.

At Twycross we were very successful in breeding our own Pot-Bellied Pigs – with one exception. When one of our elderly females produced only one piglet and was too frail after the birth to feed it, it was John Voce, by then our curator, who took the job of hand-rearing Piglet alongside four tiger cubs already in his care. At first, Piglet could only drink from a small syringe while the tiger cubs drank goats' milk out of large bottles, but within a week he had settled in and was fully convinced that he was a tiger.

As the cubs grew older he would join in all their games. While they rolled and gambolled together he would cuff them with his feet and imitate their growls with loud grunts. At mealtimes he would even sample some of their fresh meat, totally oblivious to the fact that when they were older they would be quite happy to eat *him*.

His great delight was to push his way into the middle of them to go to sleep, snuggling up to their furry bodies, even allowing them to lie on top of him to bask in their warmth.

By the time they were four months old the tiger cubs had grown bigger and had claws which even in play could inflict deep scratches on their porcine friend. For his safety we decided to remove him from the group.

We hadn't bargained for his reaction, which was to squeal and cry all day until we capitulated and against our better judgement put him back with his furry friends. Their greeting was so boisterous that they bowled him over and he enjoyed every minute of the rough and tumble.

Weeks later, as the tigers' natural instincts for stalking and hunting came into play, we had to remove him permanently before he ended up as their dinner. Fortunately, although he still disapproved, his affections were directed elsewhere when we introduced him to a companion of his own kind back in Pets' Corner, where he became a firm favourite with our visitors.

CHAPTER SEVEN

Chimps and the Media

Our love affair with the media began when we had our first monkeys at the shop. Hardly a week went by without a photographer from a local paper calling to take pictures, and there was even more interest when we had the chimps and then moved to Hints, where there was a greater variety of animals to choose from. It was a mutually advantageous liaison; the press got their story, we profited from the publicity and it was great fun. Sue and Mickey were always delighted to entertain audiences with a chimps' tea party and were often photographed tucking into tea and cakes, enjoying all the attention.

It was an innocent diversion and it never entered our heads that one day it would involve us in a commercial venture. It was while we were living in the flat above the pet shop that I saw an animal programme on BBC television that prompted me to pluck up the courage to ask if they might like to film our chimps. A lady with a typically refined BBC voice took my call and I got the distinct impression that she felt that filming chimps was rather beneath them. She reluctantly passed me on to a production assistant on a children's programme, who agreed to send a cameraman to take a film of Sue and Mickey at bathtime.

We were very excited at the prospect of our chimps appearing on television and even the bored-looking cameraman who arrived could not damp our enthusiasm. He duly set up his cameras in our old-fashioned bathroom where a warm bath already topped up with foam was ready for the moment that a delighted Sue and Mickey obligingly climbed in and began splashing bubbles at each other and at him.

When he was satisfied he had some good shots they climbed out, dried themselves with big towels and, followed by the cameraman, went downstairs where they were filmed having tea with us.

Despite the cameraman's reservations and the BBC's haughtiness, it was a lovely film for children and although our animals were filmed many times after that, no other film or appearance gave us such a thrill as that television début of our two beloved chimps.

Their début took place in 1963, a time when supermarkets were opening up all over the country, setting a new trend, cutting the price of everything including pet foods, and thereby putting many small shops out of business. We were no exception in suffering a distinct loss of trade which, with the number of animals we now had, put a terrible strain on our finances. Amazingly enough, just as we were despairing about the future it was those very supermarkets, together with the media, that came to our aid.

Fate stepped in when the Brooke Bond Tea company took a stand at the *Boys' and Girls' Exhibition* at Olympia and booked Billy Smart's chimps to do a tea party as their main attraction. They had overlooked one problem, however: rival circus owner Bertram Mills owned the sole performing rights to Olympia and refused to allow Billy Smart's chimps into the hall. Desperate to find a replacement as the chimps' tea party had been extensively advertised, the directors of Brooke Bond, spotting zoologist and TV personality George Cansdale on another stand, asked his advice.

George had no hesitation in recommending us, knowing that although our chimps were perfectly capable of carrying out a fine performance they were still essentially pet chimps who would offer no commercial threat to Bertram Mills.

He was right. Bertram Mills *did* agree to let us appear, with the stipulation that I use only one chimp and that he did not perform any other tricks.

I decided to use a very tame and amiable chimp called Johnny, who loved children. Johnny had been given to us by our good friends Cyril and Marion Grace, who made regular trips to Africa to bring back apes, monkeys and other animals for British zoos. It was on one of these excursions that they had come across Johnny, who had been the pet of some Syrians from a very early age. Cyril and Marion took an immediate fancy to the little fellow and bought him for their own special pet; with Johnny as their companion they travelled many hundreds of miles on safari in search of other animals.

Such was the bond between them that, when the time came to return to the UK, there was no question but that Johnny would come with them. By the time they arrived back in England with their collection of wild animals they were almost totally broke, without even enough money to buy petrol to get them home.

At the cheap and cheerful bed and breakfast farmhouse where they stayed overnight they confided their plight to their host, and the farmer was so captivated by the friendly chimp that he offered to buy him. It was a heart-wrenching decision, but with no other means of raising some cash until they sold their other animals, Cyril and Marion reluctantly parted with Johnny.

During the following months they missed the lovable chimp who had been such a devoted companion and, once they had sold their consignment of animals, they decided to go back to the farm to see how Johnny was faring. Their reunion was not as they anticipated. They were horrified to find their little friend chained outside with only a Labrador dog for company. Johnny recognised them immediately and made a great fuss of them, but it was pathetic to see the intelligent, sociable animal confined to an outhouse with no company or stimulation. Like so many others who are initially captivated by these lovely creatures, the farmer had neither the patience nor the time to give Johnny the attention he needed and had grown increasingly aggravated when the chimp displayed his natural instincts to climb up and swing from everything including curtains and furniture.

To the farmer's relief they offered to buy him back, took him home and then rang us to announce: 'We have got this marvellous chimp and he is just the one for you.'

They were right, he *was* delightful and because he had been brought up with children we were able to invite little ones up to have a tea party with him or play on a slide with him and join in the kind of children's games they would play at a real tea party.

Johnny was definitely the ideal chimp to put on the polished performance that Brooke Bond wanted. When the time came, he climbed happily into the little outfit that the company supplied and loved every minute of being driven in one of their tea vans into Olympia, to be given a reception by the audience almost equal to those normally reserved for royalty.

The popularity of this performance impressed the directors of Brooke Bond and we were summoned to a meeting in London at their headquarters in Cannon Street when they asked us copious questions about the set-up at Hints and talked about us being able to earn up to £100 a week using our chimps to open new supermarkets and make TV commercials. We tried to appear calm, managing to hide just how much this offer meant to us. A hundred pounds was the make or break point for us to survive.

They stressed that if we were given the contract, our chimps would have to behave impeccably, be well-dressed and cared for, as they would be ambassadors for the company in full view of a large public.

I had no qualms about assuring them that there would be no problems in that direction; being pets and not circus animals, our chimps knew how to behave in society and had excellent manners. Before making a decision, Sid Hoare, who was in charge of the company's supermarket promotions, asked if the directors could visit Hints, and although we were nervous we instantly agreed.

On the day of their arrival we were very formal and served them our favourite China tea from delicate porcelain cups. It was only later when we got to know each other that Sid Hoare teased us by pointing out that, despite trying to create a good impression, we had boobed by not serving them with their famous PG Tips!

Any faux pas we made was fortunately overshadowed by the performance of our chimps, who saved the day by winning the hearts of the directors and a twelve-month contract. An insulated van with two sleeping compartments was provided so that the chimps and ourselves could travel in style over the hundreds of miles we would clock up during the next year. The company also supplied us with masses of clothes for the chimps which they greeted with delight – and happily wore anything from bowler hats and pin-striped suits to formal dresses with picture hats, traditional Scottish kilts, policemen's uniforms, maids' outfits and football strips.

It was the most hectic year we had ever had, with me travelling all over the country with our two stars, Johnny and Rosie, opening supermarkets from Lands End to John O' Groats accompanied by Renee Carley or one of the other girls, while Nat usually held the fort at Hints. We sold the pet shop and concentrated on our two projects, the collection at Hints and our new career doing promotions.

Sometimes we did as many as five tea parties a week as well as opening one or two supermarkets. This all went off with great success, although I often wondered if it was the chimps who were the main attraction or the hundreds of free frozen chickens which the supermarkets gave away.

I don't know who enjoyed these performances more, the audiences or Rosie and Johnny. I only know that they only had to catch a glimpse of the waiting van and they would hoot with excitement.

Showing off their skills was nothing new to them. As youngsters they had been taught to ride a bike, swing on a swing, scoot along on a scooter or play on a slide. Anyone who thinks it is wrong to teach them such things should be there to see the joy of achievement on a chimp's face when it has mastered the art of cycling up our yard. The joy matches that of any child.

And, of course, the chimps differ in their grasp of things and their abilities, just like children do. I well remember the difficulty Nat had in trying to teach Johnny to walk on stilts. No matter how hard he tried, he just could not master the technique and would topple off time and again. In the end Nat resorted to getting up on the stilts herself, strutting up and down to show him. When she got up on to the stilts, raising her height by another three feet, Johnny's eyes almost stood out on stalks as she plodded up and down the hall. When she stopped he ran over, eager to have another go, and with our help took his first tottering steps before mastering this new skill perfectly. After that we taught all our chimps to stilt-walk, with Nat giving them an initial demonstration.

In those days learning and playing was part of their life. Each day opened new horizons for them and a new experience. How many chimps have walked over the Scottish moors, stayed in the best hotels and even travelled across the Atlantic in a jet, or over to Jersey in a potato boat as ours have done?

There was one memorable occasion when Nat was travelling on her own with Rosie to do a promotion in Scotland. As they were making good time, Nat decided to stop off and have a picnic in the woods with Rosie, who just adored eating *alfresco*. When the meal was finished and Nat decided to wash the van down before continuing their journey, Rosie helped her to carry buckets of water from a nearby brae and had joined her in sponging the vehicle when a car suddenly appeared on the Highland road and almost ran off course when its occupants spotted the bizarre scene.

Rosie was undoubtedly one of the most intelligent and good-natured chimps we have ever had. She recognised every hotel we stayed in and when we revisited our usual hotel in Norwich, would remember the room we had previously stayed in and would pull me down the corridor until we came to the door. Once inside she would pick up the phone to reception and would order tea with some very expressive grunting, which by now the girl on the other end recognised, and bread and butter would duly arrive.

On another occasion, having to stay over at a very select hotel, Rosie stayed in the room and slept in the bed with me. In the morning, while I was only half-awake, a waiter came in with tea which he placed at our bedside, then turning to Rosie, who was just waking up, he said, straight-faced: 'And what would Madam like for breakfast?'

Even when Rosie sat up and stared at him he did not bat an eyelid.

'Madam will have fruit salad, please,' I said, equally seriously. 'And I will have bacon and egg.'

When we moved to Twycross our chimps' promotional career continued and they even broke into movies.

Because of her wonderful temperament Rosie was chosen to appear in a Hammer Horror film with actor Peter Cushing, in which she played an ape who turned savage. It was hilarious, because there was supposed to be a close-up of this monster ape eating raw meat with the blood running down her face, and there was no way that any chimp would be persuaded to eat raw meat. In the end we had to fake it by dying a large pineapple blood red to get the right effect.

Unlike most of the other chimps, Rosie would carry out instructions not just from myself but from Nat, Dorothy Phillips and Renee Carley as well, so that while I was busy with a particularly important promotion it was Renee who spent six weeks with her at Shepperton Studios when she co-starred in a film with Hattie Jacques and Leslie Phillips, called *In the Dog House*.

There was only one occasion when she misbehaved

during filming; it was in Eton, when a car had to screech to a halt behind her as she cycled down a street. Everything went like clockwork until Rosie heard the squeal of the car's brakes, which frightened her so much that she jumped off the bike and ran straight through the open door of a nearby house.

Renee dashed after her and arrived to find Rosie sitting next to the owner happily watching television. The poor man was too frightened to move.

During her six weeks of stardom Rosie became a real favourite at the studios and struck up such a bond with Hattie Jacques that a year later, when the actress was the subject of *This is Your Life*, Rosie was the surprise guest and, wearing a new dress, ran straight across the stage to Hattie and threw her arms round her.

Another chimp called Lucy, who always had a mischievous streak in her, also became a film star. There was one scene in a film where Margaret Rutherford, the legendary actress who played the first Miss Marple, had to wash Lucy's face with a face cloth as she gave her a bath. Lucy was quite happy to be washed until it came to her face – and no matter how many times Margaret Rutherford tried to do it, Lucy would snatch the flannel from her and triumphantly drop it in the bath. Time and again the scene was repeated, with Lucy disposing of dozens of face cloths, wasting valuable filming time while I was more concerned that she might bite her famous co-star. Instead Lucy finally became so bored with the game that she capitulated and allowed her face to be washed so that the scene was successfully in the can.

I thought this was a minor hiccup but it seemed that Lucy was *not* destined for a career in the movies, as became apparent when she was hired to appear in a film being made at MGM Studios starring Cornel Wilde and Rhonda Fleming. The moment she went on to the film set she saw an open pot of paint and, before anyone could intervene, stuck her arm into it so that shooting had to be delayed for hours while I cleaned pints of bright green paint off her long hairy arms.

The scene where she had to sit on the bed and wake Cornel Wilde up was hours late, and although Lucy sailed through it like a true pro, it was the end of her short-lived career as a movie star.

Johnny also made his début in films when he appeared with Terry-Thomas in an Ealing comedy where they both had to walk down a London street wearing identical bowler hats and pin-striped suits, carrying briefcases. With so many public appearances behind him, unlike the rather temperamental females of the species Johnny performed the scene as though he had been acting all his life.

Johnny was one of the most adaptable chimps. He even learned to ride a small motor-bike and sidecar, which brought him a very special booking to appear at the Military Tattoo at White City, when he sat astride a 1000cc motor-bike and drove it round and round the arena to the applause of a crowd of thousands, who roared with laughter as I, dressed as a policewoman, ran around after him in a vain attempt to arrest him. They had no idea that it was in fact Renee Carley, hidden from view in the sidecar, who controlled and steered the machine.

We had another delightful little chimp called Sam, who was short and thick-set, and we used to say to him, 'Sam Small. Not very tall, at all.' And he would smile mischievously at us and raise his eyebrows. He never forgot that jingle and the same expression would come over his face when we recited it years later.

Poor little Sam was not as versatile as Johnny and no matter how hard he tried he just could not master the art of riding a bicycle. Even with Nat's infinitely patient coaching, crawling round with him trying to get him balanced, he was a total flop. Until one day outside a Sheffield supermarket where we were making an appearance for Brooke Bond I had an idea.

The store was on a slope and I put Sam on a bike and began to roll him gently down the hill and then let go. As he gained momentum he began to pedal and the look of sheer delight that came over his face at his achievement was a joy to see. After that he became one of our best cyclists.

However, when we made the advert for Brooke Bond entitled *The Tour de France*, the scene was shot with the bicycle mounted on the back of a truck so the chimp did not even have to pedal. The public loved it.

Over the years we all had a lot of fun, despite it being very hard work. The revenue earned by the chimps was invaluable; it helped to subsidise the animals at Twycross and the new buildings that were necessary if we were to improve the zoo and the chimps' own standard of living.

CHAPTER EIGHT

Chimps and the Media II

The chimps enjoyed all the travelling and the razzmatazz but I often longed to be back at the zoo instead of being marooned in hotel rooms in strange towns. I rang Twycross frequently, craving for news but comforted by the knowledge that I was playing a vital part in keeping it financially afloat.

Sometimes our new showbiz connections did have their compensations, like being invited to take part with a chimp in the *Daily Mail* Atlantic Air Race from the GPO Tower to the top of the Empire State Building in New York. Any means of transport could be used, the only stipulation being that competitors should cross the Atlantic either on scheduled flights or in their own plane. After clocking in at the GPO Tower, competitors were free to choose their own means of transport to the airport, and amongst the vehicles used were helicopters, bicycles, even horse-drawn carriages.

Brooke Bond were enthusiastic about one of the chimps taking part and although I was nervous about flying I agreed to take Tina, a very good-natured but large chimp who already weighed around 60 lb. Because of her size I insisted that Dorothy Phillips should join the party, which also included Brooke Bond executives. A special dispensation had to be granted to allow Tina up the GPO Tower where she behaved perfectly, holding my hand in the lift and waiting patiently to have her clock card punched before we raced back to the lift and down to the Rolls-Royce which was waiting to take us to the airport.

Wearing a silver space suit, Tina settled down in the front passenger seat posing for the sea of press photographers who surrounded the limousine, while Dorothy and I sat in the back praying she would not turn round and take a bite out of the exquisite beige leather upholstery.

Tina certainly was the star of the show, at least until we were ready to board a VC10 at Heathrow Airport, where we removed her silver space suit and packed her unceremoniously into a travelling box. Although we had pleaded with airline officials, they were not prepared to allow a chimp to occupy a passenger seat so Tina travelled in the hold with the luggage.

Eight hours later when we arrived at Kennedy Airport, Tina was retrieved from the ignominious cabin in the hold and dressed once more in her space suit to meet the waiting press. On alighting from the plane we were greeted by a truly amazing sight. A table stood on the runway complete with a lace tablecloth, a silver tea service and delicate bone china cups for the benefit of the waiting photographers. With extreme dignity Tina sat down at the table and allowed a waiter to pour the tea before genteelly sipping from the cups with all the aplomb of a true VIP.

Once the pictures had been taken we raced to Customs, only to meet with another delay: they refused to allow Tina's supply of bananas into the country. Our chimp did the sensible thing – she ate the lot! Then we were on our way once more, racing to the Empire State Building in a white Cadillac driven by a uniformed chauffeur, with Tina waving to the cheering crowds.

She entered the lift and ascended to the top of the tallest building in the world and handed her card over to be stamped amid rousing cheers from the assembled reporters and press photographers. This reception proved too much for Tina. Overcome by the occasion she wet her pants and had to retire to the ladies' powder room. Washed and changed, she was ready to meet her admiring audience, and when the press requested a photograph of her sitting on the balcony of the Empire State Building she was happy to oblige. Why not? King Kong had done it all before, so with complete composure she happily perched on the rail silhouetted against New York's skyscraper skyline.

No, we did not win the air race but we received more publicity than any of the other entrants. During our four-day sightseeing tour in New York we were fêted wherever we went. Our Cadillac was followed by a cavalcade of press and TV photographers, for even blasé New Yorkers had never seen a chimp in a space suit riding round in a stretch limo before.

By the time we arrived at Kennedy Airport to make our journey home we were exhausted but elated and had to face another battery of press before our departure on a VC10. Tina posed graciously for the cameras like the celebrity she had become. But her composure soon changed when she was bundled unceremoniously into her travelling box and wheeled off to the hold; her face contorted with outrage, her screams of anger could be heard as she disappeared to join the rest of the freight.

At Heathrow there were no waiting pressmen or crowds to greet us and we were able to slip quietly away to a nearby hotel. That night, in our room, Tina put her arm affectionately around my neck and snuggled up. I think she too had realised that the price of fame was too high and was only too happy to return to the normality of a zoo.

Travelling with Tina and the other chimps increased my affection and admiration for them. They were wonderful companions and I came to realise how very sensitive they could be to one's moods, just how much they understood and how very loyal they could be to anyone closely associated with them. I felt privileged to have been able to become so close to them and realised that they should be treated with the respect they deserve. By all means laugh with them, but never *at* them.

During the eighteen years in which our chimps starred in

television commercials and promotions for Brooke Bond, they made a valuable contribution to the zoo's finances, enabling us to buy other animals and to build more modern housing. It was they who were responsible for our sea-lion pool, for when a local manufacturer of mechanical diggers wanted one of our chimps to pose on his machine for publicity purposes, we agreed – providing they dug us out a sea-lion pool.

It was Tina again who starred, together with three other chimps, in a twenty-minute film entitled *The Golfer's Progress*. It included shots of the chimps playing golf and became so popular that golf clubs all over the country bought it.

In the film, Tina had to be given golf lessons by an instructor played by myself. There was no problem teaching her to swing the club and hit the ball, but it wasn't so easy to get out of the way. I soon changed tactics after I had received a cracking blow on the head, and made Tina take up position and wait until I ran clear, when I could shout, 'Go on, hit it!' Then she would drive off like a real pro.

It became obvious that although Tina was quite capable of learning to take a swing at the ball, it was almost impossible to teach her the difference between an exuberant thump and a delicate putt. In the end another chimp was recruited to take over in that area.

When the two chimps had become sufficiently proficient they were taken on location to the local golf course at Ashby. Less able but enthusiastic golfers are known as 'rabbits', and to illustrate this, in the script a rabbit was supposed to pop up just as Tina was about to tee off.

We had two rescued hand-reared hares at the zoo and this seemed to be the ideal situation to release them back to Nature. All went to plan until we let the first hare out. Tina was lining up at the tee when she spotted it and she immediately took off after it, clutching her golf club, followed by the rest of the chimps with Dorothy, Jenny and me in hot pursuit. Only when the hare had disappeared over the horizon did we manage to retrieve the chimps and resume filming.

Tina had always been Jenny Minney's favourite chimp and when she announced that she was getting married she insisted that Tina must be her bridesmaid. A very startled but amiable vicar gave Tina his blessing and she duly arrived at the church in a frilly bridesmaid's dress especially made for the occasion, then proceeded to steal the limelight from the bride and groom, posing for pictures and helping to cut the cake before having to be taken home slightly tipsy from sipping champagne. It certainly was an unusual wedding, but a very happy day for Jenny and her new husband – and, of course, for their 'bridesmaid'.

Filming another TV commercial with Johnny proved extremely nerve-wracking. I had to take the chimps to London to be measured by a famous costumier for outfits, which included evening suits, togas and cowboy outfits. Johnny, dressed in a cowboy outfit with leather chaps, gun belt and six-shooter, was to fling back saloon doors in John Wayne style, draw his gun and shoot. Over and over again we rehearsed it, with me standing in front of him to give him the signal. A quick learner, Johnny was quite happy to oblige, except that when we were in front of the camera he was so quick on the draw that I could not get off the set before the camera homed in. Time and again we went over it just to get one shot, with Johnny getting quicker while I became slower and slower.

Frustrated, we took a well-earned break and decided to have one more attempt: if that failed, the whole script would have to be changed. I was so determined that this time it would succeed that as soon as I gave Johnny the signal I dived sideways on to the floor out of camera range and they captured the perfect shot.

By now we had become acutely aware that there was a time limit on the chimps being able to perform in public. Once they reach sexual maturity they are no longer safe to go amongst the public. At six or seven years old when the females begin to come into season they become completely unpredictable and it is virtually impossible to control them, so at this age they have to be withdrawn from public life.

Male chimps mature more slowly and usually remain fairly co-operative until they are eight or nine years old before they are, in our case, retired to the zoo. Once they grow big and develop huge arms and chests and weigh up to 100 lb they no longer look acceptable dressed up.

Many of our original chimps, including Johnny, were reaching maturity and we realised how difficult it would be for those animals who had led such a varied existence, being spoiled, fussed and the centre of attention, to adjust to a more sedate existence in the zoo – even though we hoped they would eventually be integrated into a family group where they might breed. Inevitably for the chimps who had been in the limelight, to now live in a cage, no matter how luxurious it might be with underfloor heating and an outdoor run, is nowhere near as stimulating as being in the outside world.

We desperately needed to build a better Chimp House and we approached Brooke Bond to ask if they would donate money for a new building to house their former stars. We proposed a Chimp House that would benefit the company, combining a luxury home for the chimps with an educational history of tea, displaying the costumes the chimps had worn in the television commercials together with video footage of their performances.

Sid Hoare was enthusiastic but our timing was wrong. Brooke Bond had merged with the Oxo company and the new management felt no allegiance to the chimps and was far from enthusiastic about using them in the future.

The bubble had burst, as I knew it would. We had not expected the chimps' TV slot to last for ever. They could still entertain crowds at the zoo with tea parties, while I could at last put the lonely nights in hotel rooms and constant travelling behind me and look forward to concentrating on the zoo.

Johnny, now reaching maturity, would soon have to be retired. Already he was becoming over-possessive about me and would grunt a warning if anyone came near me or touched me.

Like other mature chimps, Johnny's behaviour combined with his mental ability made him a formidable opponent for any new keeper and he could make their lives a misery. He would throw dirt at them, spit at them and refuse to let them unlock the sliding doors. He was also an adept opportunist, stealing a keeper's possessions or any of the kitchen equipment, hiding it in his nest, tormenting the frustrated keeper until I, Nat or Dorothy had to be called to persuade him to hand it over.

Realising the importance of being able to retrieve objects from the apes, we had taught them from an early age to 'swap' the items for something more desirable, like an ice cream or chocolate bar. Instilling swapping at an early age enabled us to take back any dangerous object, like a metal button which they could swallow. Of course, a swap must always be worthwhile in the receiver's eyes. You must never doublecross them. The chimps are too clever not to know when they are being cheated.

It was now our responsibility to repay the chimps who had made such an important contribution to the finances of Twycross by giving them the best care and as much stimulation as we could devise so that they could adjust happily to their new lives. We still gave them old clothes to play with, hid sweets and other treats in boxes and jars around their enclosures, gave them toys and installed TV sets in their quarters. Even so, whenever they heard the car they would hoot loudly, thinking they were going out, and when that didn't materialise, they would then go quiet or sulk in a corner with disappointment.

If we were to continue with our tea parties and any other public appearances, we knew that we would have to buy some new young chimps to take over from our old-stagers. They should preferably be under the age of twelve months if we were to be sure they would adapt to living away from the family group. For once chimps have become accustomed to living in groups of their own kind and have learned to depend on each other, they never truly learn to depend on humans in the same way and will never trust them.

The only other chimps we could consider as replacements to our seasoned performers were older chimps that had been brought up as pets and had bonded with humans. This was never really a practical alternative because many of them, due to their early experiences, were left with memories of not being able to trust human beings. They usually had a nervous streak that made them unsuitable candidates for public performances, unlike the youngsters we had handled ourselves.

At a very young age chimps thoroughly enjoy learning and have no inhibitions about showing their enjoyment or displeasure. If they are upset, their voices get very loud and they can scream like a child; even though they don't shed tears you cannot mistake their feelings. When they are elated, especially when they have learned a new skill, they are equally vocal in showing their pleasure.

Chimps respond to the amount of effort you are prepared to give. Ours were always taught to be obedient from the earliest age. Treated in the same manner as a small child, we taught them table manners by making them sit at a table to drink a cup of tea or eat a boiled egg. If they tried to climb down from the table they were corrected and brought back just as Mum would correct an infant. Chimps, like children, respond equally to praise and correction and they were almost as proud of their achievements as we were.

That is why it saddens me when people describe giving them the opportunity to expand their experiences and horizons by teaching them skills as *exploitation*. Or when I hear the latest philosophy in some world zoos that animals should be treated as animals and there should be no personal contact or communication – they should be left to their own devices.

If this is the way of the future, I will never agree with it and I don't think the chimps would either. I have been privileged to have been closely associated with them and know that my life has been enriched by their presence and I am close enough to them to recognise their appreciation of the stimulation we have given.

Zoo directors had warned us that because we had treated our male chimps so much like humans, they would never breed. We dismissed their pessimistic prophecies, but as time passed they were proved right. Whatever the reason, Sam had no interest in the female chimps and Johnny's sexual activities had been cut short as a baby when he was castrated in Africa. Their total disinterest caused great frustration amongst the females when they came into season, and they were bad-tempered and fractious.

We were half-heartedly considering a solution when one day a very excitable, strange little foreign gentleman arrived in tears on our doorstep with a chimp called Oscar. When he had calmed down enough to tell us his sad story it turned out that for six years Oscar had lived the life of a circus and cabaret star, travelling in a luxury trailer dining on the best food and drinking the best wines. Now at eight years old he was becoming too unpredictable to continue his career touring the clubs and his owner was faced with finding him a good home or having him put down.

'I cannot bear it,' he sobbed, grabbing my hand. 'Please, take Oscar in and give him a good home.'

I pulled my hand away. 'I am very sorry but we've got more than enough chimps. We just couldn't cope with another adult.'

'But if you don't have him he will have to be put down and that would break my heart. Oscar is a very fine chimp. You won't regret it. He will make you babies.'

I thought he was talking rubbish but his distress was so genuine that Nat and I did not have the heart to turn him away.

When we agreed to take Oscar his thanks were so profuse that I had to hold up my hand to stop the flow. 'We will have him on a month's trial,' I told him firmly. 'If he doesn't settle in then you must have him back.'

'Thank you, thank you,' he said, kissing mine and Nat's hands. 'You wait and see, Oscar will make you many babies.' This was his parting shot as he almost ran down the drive, leaving us with yet another chimp.

Two weeks later, Oscar's owner was proved right. Oscar not only settled in but mated with Sue, a very sophisticated female chimp who strangely enough had a similar background to her suitor in that she had done the rounds of public appearances. Sue conceived immediately and so Oscar earned his place at the zoo as a stud chimp.

Sceptics once more gave a gloomy forecast when they heard that one of our celebrity chimps was pregnant. How could a chimp that had been hand-reared and brought up with humans possibly know how to look after an infant?

Determined to prove them wrong and to ensure that everything would go smoothly, we added a small extension to the Chimp House consisting of two bedrooms with underfloor heating. In this we installed a camp bed so that Dorothy Phillips and I could take it in turns to sleep there during the last month of Sue's pregnancy.

We slept in the passageway outside Sue's bedroom, and although puzzled by our presence, she shared our flasks of tea and joined us companionably in watching the programmes on our portable television set. Religiously we kept our nightly vigil but after six weeks nothing had happened.

Then, on a day when I was out and it was Dorothy's day off, the day keeper looked in on Sue and found her with a newly born baby, a gorgeous three and a half pounds male, who was already suckling at his mother's breast.

Sue proved the sceptics wrong by being an extremely capable mother. Whether it was because of her early days when she had played with dolls and children's toys, or from her observation of human mothers with babies, instead of carrying her baby around with her like a normal chimp she made a nest from her wood and wool bedding and pushed him around the floor in it like a pram.

We called our very first chimp baby 'Brooke' after the tea company, and after a time we allowed Oscar to integrate with Sue and his offspring. Oscar readily adopted the role of father, showing great interest in Brooke, but Sue kept a watchful eye on him, ready to intervene if his play became too rough and only allowing him to have contact with the baby for short intervals.

Brooke's birth opened up a whole new world of experience for the other chimps, who took great delight in the baby and enormous interest in each stage of his development. Sue's female counterparts would look after him, making sure that the more boisterous young chimps kept their distance as first he learned to crawl and then with Sue's help took his first tentative steps. As he grew older they were allowed to play with him while the other, older males acted as uncles.

Our very firstborn chimp baby was one of the few apes that we bred that did not have to come into the house – a triumph in itself.

Unfortunately, Brooke's life came to a tragic end. When he was adult we were asked by another zoo if we could supply them with an adult male chimp to go on breeding loan and reluctantly we agreed to send Brooke.

The outside chimp enclosure at his new home had a water moat and one day, possibly chased by the other chimps, he fell in and drowned. We vowed never to have a water moat around any of our enclosures, only dry ditches with brick walls and glass panels. It also made us reconsider loaning out any other chimps in the future.

CHAPTER NINE

A Tall Story

She stands fourteen feet high with a coat patterned like velvet crazy paving, long slender legs and a delicate head with huge soft brown eyes. What is she? A giraffe, of course.

Except that our very first giraffe did not look anything like this. It had taken months of searching, contacting dealers and zoos, to locate a young female. In the end it was Jimmy Chipperfield who happened to have one he had just imported that he offered to us for what we considered to be the enormous sum of £650. Normally we could not even have considered it, had it not been for some friends, who had helped us in the past by making labels for the cages, offering to donate some money towards the purchase.

We arrived at the Chipperfield farm in Southampton brimming with anticipation, but our first sight of the giraffe filled us with dismay. She was completely moth-eaten and had no hair on her tail. But beggars can't be choosers and, having been assured that the missing hair would grow, we clinched the deal.

If finding a giraffe had proved difficult, it was nothing compared to the incredible problems we had in transporting her. It had not occurred to us that by the time a giraffe standing fourteen feet high had been loaded on to a trailer she was almost twenty feet off the ground! It took us a week to work out a suitable route avoiding low bridges and any other obstacles, but with the help of the AA we managed it. Even so, for part of the journey she had to be accompanied by a police car, and several overhead telephone cables had to be taken down by BT engineers to enable the truck with its precious cargo to pass underneath.

When she arrived at the zoo in a twenty-foot crate she had her head sticking out of the back watching the cavalcade of press cars and intrigued families out for the day who tagged on behind. One man had even made a fifty-mile detour to follow the giraffe. Our newcomer had certainly attracted national publicity and had brought her own followers to the zoo.

I was so excited I couldn't wait for her to be unloaded and fetched a ladder to lean against the side of the truck so that I could climb up and see her. It was breathtaking to look into the long-lashed eyes of this shy, delicate creature who seemed to be taking everything in her stride.

'Oh, Nat. She is beautiful,' I said in awe.

We had already decided on her name. She would be called Sorbo, after the friends who had donated the money, and she was the largest animal we had ever owned.

We followed Sorbo and the truck to the place we had designated as her home, a very large old barn with a corrugated iron roof which had been used to store hay and straw. It was an extremely ugly building but the only one that stood twenty feet high and could easily be converted into a Giraffe House. We had already installed a walkthrough for visitors, which was separated from the two indoor pens by metal bars. Onto this we had built an outdoor enclosure with chainlink fencing and a dry ditch into which we planned to unload the giraffe and I felt a flutter of nerves wondering how this highly-strung creature would cope when she walked down the ramp into her new quarters.

I need not have worried. Once the trailer was drawn up to the enclosure we lowered the ramp and allowed Sorbo to get her bearings before she attempted to negotiate her way backwards out of the crate. I was afraid that if she panicked she could slip and injure herself on the ramp, but after carefully taking two steps backwards she came out like a perfectly balanced, well trained racehorse, turning her long neck to take in her new surroundings.

Any qualms we may have harboured that a giraffe might be difficult to keep were dispelled within the first few weeks. In fact, their needs are very much like those of horses, so with our background knowledge of equines we were able to cope with her diet, which consisted mainly of lucerne hay or clover which had to come by special delivery all the way from the east coast, plus a mix containing bran, oats, maize, pellets and locust beans. The main difference between the giraffe and horses was the height of her hayrack, which was lodged about fifteen feet up on the wall.

It had never been our intention to keep a solitary giraffe and after twelve months, when Sorbo was beginning to develop into a mature cow, we started to look around for a young bull giraffe as a mate. These were far from easy to come by but we knew that Chester Zoo did have one and we approached its founder, George Mottershead, to see if he would part with his animal, only to be told that he could not spare him. We seemed to have come to a dead end until months later we had a call from George, who had relented and offered us Gerry, a magnificent two-and-a-half-year-old bull giraffe who was already seventeen feet tall and growing.

This time we knew the ropes about having a giraffe on the move and again with the help of the AA the route from Chester was organised and Gerry duly arrived with a police escort and the press in hot pursuit.

Gerry was placed in the indoor pen next to Sorbo to effect an introduction. For such a large animal, Gerry was kindness itself and took to Sorbo immediately and to his new surroundings. There was nothing nervous about his temperament and he would quite happily play to the crowds, making soft noises as if talking to them and allowing anyone tall enough to stroke his nose.

Venturing into the unknown with our two protégées.

Hints where it all began. (John Doidge)

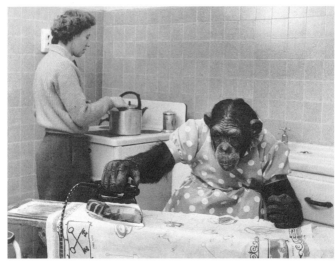

'I'm a genius at ironing!'

Comedy Hour with Noddy and Choppers. (John Doidge)

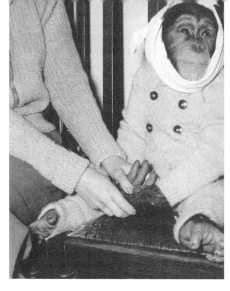

Even a chimp can have a toothache. Johnny after having a tooth extracted.

Tina as bridesmaid at Jenny Minney's wedding. (John Doidge)

Keeper Dorothy Phillips has a near miss from Johnny and Rosie – Hints Lane. (John Doidge)

All aboard for Twycross Zoo. (*Daily Mirror*)

TV presenter Jean Morton shares the limelight with Rosie to open Twycross Zoo in 1963. (John Doidge)

Tickets please. Johnny greets visitors on opening day. What prices! (John Doidge)

Renee Carley acts as nursemaid to baby elephant Iris who joined staff in the house for lunch. (John Doidge)

Molly welcoming Sorbo the first giraffe to Twycross. (John Doidge)

Nightwatch. Renee Carley keeping vigil awaiting birth of first giraffe baby, Domino. (John Doidge)

Winter Wonderland. Tina with John and helper
after a snowstorm.

Sam Man digging out our first sea lion pool. (JCB)

Victory. (John Doidge)

Rosie and Norman
Wisdom share a private
moment.

He also took a great liking to Juno, our Great Dane, and would lick the top of her head with his eighteen-inches-long blue tongue.

Visitors found these stately animals fascinating. Giraffes are ungulates – the tallest hoofed land mammals, characterised by their ability to move at fast speed and vegetarian diet.

Living ungulates are divided into odd-toed, which include horses, tapirs and rhinos, and even-toed, of which examples at Twycross include Giraffes, Batrian Camels, Alpacas and Zebu Cattle.

The giraffes are by far the most spectacular, with their huge frame and long neck which stretches to approximately six feet and which enables them to reach high branches. Like humans, they have seven vertebrae in their neck, but whereas ours are about half an inch long, the giraffe's neck bones are ten inches long.

They are ruminants with complex chambered stomachs with a rumen in which to store food until it can be chewed in comfort. Visitors are always fascinated to watch them chewing the cud, which involves them rechewing food that has already been swallowed.

The food is regurgitated from the stomach back into the mouth, where it is chewed again before being transferred back into the stomach in the way that cows, sheep and goats deal with their food.

The difference with the giraffe is that because its neck is so long and lanky you can clearly see the balls of food travelling up and down. These animals never ceased to amaze me and are amongst the most popular with zoo visitors.

Our giraffe couple had such presence that whenever I drove past and saw them walking elegantly around their enclosure I caught my breath in wonder. A year later when they mated we thought our dreams had come true.

It was Renee Carley with her amazing empathy with animals who built up a very special relationship with the giraffes and it was she who clucked around like a mother hen when they mated and we knew there was a baby giraffe on the way.

We had fourteen and a half months to wait for the birth, but because we could not be certain of the date of conception, Renee insisted on sleeping in the Giraffe House for six weeks before the estimated date of delivery. With her camp bed and a television set for entertainment, she took up residence in the House to keep a nightly vigil, while the two giraffes looked on in amazement from their respective pens.

Although Nat and I had been present at the birth of many foals, giraffes, because of their shape, size and temperament, presented unique problems.

As giraffes are the tallest land mammals, a newly-born giraffe falls into the world from a great height, an alarming six or seven feet. We prepared for this by providing a deep bed of straw in Sorbo's quarters; nevertheless it was a frightening prospect, particularly should there be any complications during the birth.

Typically, Sorbo decided to calve during the night and the first we knew of this was Renee banging on the door to make sure we did not miss the event. I scrambled out of bed and pulled on trousers, sweater and anorak and joined Nat to sprint across to the Giraffe House, terrified we might miss even one second of the birth.

We watched with bated breath as Sorbo strained with each contraction until first the forelegs and the nose appeared; another contraction and more effort from Sorbo and the baby was literally ejected to fall head-first on to the peat below. It was alarming to watch and hard to believe that a newborn could survive that kind of entry into the world without being damaged. We looked on helplessly at the gangly legs and long neck of the calf threshing around, and we willed it to be all right.

We were powerless to go to its aid as it made its first attempts to rise, the long neck weaving from side to side as it tried to balance itself. But Nature has designed newly-born giraffes to stand and be able to run soon after birth in order to escape the many predators who normally threaten them in the wild.

As onlookers, to watch the calf staggering round the cage looking as if she would break her legs or her neck was extremely traumatic, but Nature triumphed in the end when she managed to balance herself and tottered over to her mother to begin to suckle.

In the wild it is not unusual for a group of giraffe to stand in a circle around a pregnant cow whilst she gives birth, which acts as protection for Mum and Baby from other marauding animals. In this case Gerry did not have to perform these duties but observed the birth from his adjacent pen, leaning over to take a closer look at his beautifully marked calf who turned out, to our joy, to be female.

Dawn was breaking as we left the Giraffe House and gibbons whooped a chorus to accompany us back to the house. Elation had overtaken fatigue and together with Renee we ate a substantial breakfast and swapped ideas for names, ending up with Domino because of the calf's markings. For weeks we haunted the Giraffe House, unable to take our eyes off our beautiful new addition, and Renee, who could not be dissuaded, insisted on continuing to sleep there.

A year later Sorbo conceived again, and again produced a female calf; we called her Snoopy, and she also thrived. This population explosion and the possibility of more calves to come prompted us to speed up plans for a new and larger Giraffe House and enclosure. The old Giraffe House had worked well; because of this and our limited funds we decided that we would keep the new design simple and straightforward. Plans were drawn up; the building was to be of precast sand-faced blocks, on paper a simple building exercise, but like all our building ventures there were untold disasters ahead.

It was spring when the work commenced and in a very short time the bricklayers had erected a sixty-feet-long, twelve-feet-high wall absolutely on schedule. We watched their progress with satisfaction. That night there was a force ten gale; the wind howled and trees creaked in protest. As soon as it was light, I went down with one of our keepers, Dorothy, to inspect the zoo for any damage.

We arrived at the site of the Giraffe House just in time to see our new sixty-feet wall begin to sway in the wind until it folded up like a pack of cards. I was utterly horrified. The builders had not stabilised the wall properly and now we had to start again from scratch and put up with a three-week delay while we re-ordered the special building blocks and other materials. It took an extra month before the new House was completed, with the wall now reinforced with pillars.

Once finished, it stood boldly out on the skyline with its new enclosure – a ditched paddock with a low wall to give the public an uninterrupted view of the giraffes.

The next obstacle we had to overcome was moving the four giraffes several hundred yards through the zoo to their new home. How could we do it? We could not lead them, and herding them along was fraught with danger. If one lagged behind or decided to stray off, we would lose control and have the entire group on the loose.

We decided to ask the advice of someone who had overcome this kind of problem on more than one occasion. Dick Chipperfield always had circus animals in transit. He informed us that the only way to move them safely was to hire scaffolding and build a runway from their old quarters to their new House. We took his advice, had the scaffolding erected and then bought rolls and rolls of six-foot sacking which we attached to the poles to give the runway a solid look.

Dick had also stressed upon us the importance of getting all the giraffes out of their old House and on the move down the runway together, moving in a tightly knit group and not allowing any stragglers.

I don't think any of us relished the task ahead but all the staff turned out to help and our vet Mary Brancker was on hand in case there were any accidents. Our first move was to take down part of the old run, leaving a gap which led on to the runway. A keeper stood just inside the runway tempting the giraffes with a bucket of feed. We waited patiently, knowing we could not force the giraffes out of their House. As the three females hesitatingly emerged and took their first tentative steps towards the runway, it was Gerry, our big male, who refused to budge an inch. Although his females had left him, he spent ages gazing at the gap they had gone through.

We watched helplessly as the three females who had been following the keeper stopped moving forward when they realised the male of the herd was missing. We had to persuade Gerry to follow them. Two of us grabbed some sacking and stood behind him flapping it around his legs, which did not have the desired effect but just caused him to panic and run off down the pathway. The others bolted in all directions and we stood aghast as they pushed and jostled each other. It would be a miracle if none of them was hurt.

We could only stand and watch until their panic subsided and they calmed down sufficiently to take stock. Once they realised that they were together in the safety of their herd, they all began to move on towards the new quarters with the keeper some yards ahead, and to everyone's relief they arrived at the new House intact.

Three of them went inside, but Snoopy, who had lagged behind, kicked her way through the sacking in her anxiety to join the others and plunged over the three-feet wall of the enclosure into the ditch, knocking herself unconscious.

Her huge body lay in a crumpled heap, her head and legs at a strange angle. Convinced that she was dead, caution was thrown to the wind; all the staff, Nat and myself, and our vet jumped over the wall. Yet Snoopy was still alive and I prayed that there were no limbs broken as Mary Brancker gave her an injection to stimulate her heart and began to massage her. It seemed an eternity before there was some reaction as we coaxed and heaved, trying to get her to her feet. Then suddenly she got up, kicked out ungratefully at us and trotted over to join her companions inside the new House. A cheer went up amongst the helpers and relief surged through me as we walked to the new quarters to see if the four animals were settling down.

Our giraffes had found their hay racks and were already tucking into the lush Lucerne hay, their big eyes taking in their luxury surroundings, the ceramic wall tiles which could easily be cleaned and the underfloor heating which we had provided. The place seemed to meet with their approval, and whenever I went in at night to check on them they would be lying on the floor enjoying the warmth.

Renee had tremendous empathy with the giraffes. They are nervous creatures, but with keepers who have the right temperament and understanding they do build up trust – which is vital as it is sometimes necessary to handle them to perform routine foot trimming or to carry out routine check-ups. This is why we make a point of gently getting the giraffes used to being handled when they are very young.

The value of this approach was made very clear when one of our giraffes had trouble calving. Mary Brancker, assisted by Roger Coley, was in attendance and quickly realised that instead of a normal presentation, where the calf's head rests between its two front legs, in this case the only things visible were the two legs; the head was nowhere to be seen. Sometimes a calf can be presented with its head back and the vet has to turn it into the right position before the mother is able to give birth; fortunately, in this instance, that was not the case. By now, though, after hours of straining the mother was getting very tired and we knew that the calf too must be distressed.

Ropes were fetched, and as if the giraffe knew that we were all there to help, she obligingly backed her rear end up to the bars so that the ropes could be tied around the calf's legs. As she strained with the next contraction, Roger and the zoo curator pulled on the ropes and the calf plopped out.

The ropes were quickly detached as the mother licked the calf gently and nudged it with her foot. In the wild, as I have mentioned, it is vital for the calf to get up as soon as possible because of the danger from predators, which is one of the reasons why the mother will kick the baby gently with her foot to urge it to its feet. After half an hour of struggling, our newly born calf finally stood on all four legs and began to suckle. It was a strong, healthy calf none the worse for its difficult entry into the world, and from that day Scotty, as we named him, never looked back.

At Twycross we have had great success in breeding these elegant animals, and Scotty, now twenty-four years old, is the oldest breeding bull giraffe in the country.

CHAPTER TEN

An Elephant Never Forgets

Our policy of buying only baby animals stood us in good stead when we purchased our first elephant. In the 1960s, buying a baby elephant was an easy matter as there were no restrictions on imports and dealers usually had one or two baby elephants in stock.

We soon found just what we were looking for in the back yard of a Birmingham dealer's shop – a tiny three-month-old female baby Indian elephant no bigger than a large dog, utterly irresistible with twinkling brown eyes and grey skin which was still covered in long black baby hair.

We would never have been able to afford or house a fully grown adult, but Iris, as we called her, would fit nicely into the one vacant brick building which would serve as our Elephant House, and would give us breathing space to find the money needed to build proper quarters.

The day Iris arrived at the zoo we had filled her house with thick bedding of fresh straw, which she viewed with approval. As she was so young she was still being bottle fed and settled down happily to drink her milk, trumpeting gently and rubbing her trunk up and down Renee Carley's neck as she held the bottle for her. By night-time Iris seemed to have settled in and was quite contented. It had been an exciting but exhausting day and everyone decided to go to bed early; however, loud plaintive bellowing from the Elephant House shattered any hope of a peaceful night. Lights went on in the house and Nat, Renee and I met on the stairs and rushed out to investigate.

As soon as she saw us, Iris stopped bellowing; we looked her over anxiously to see if we could find the cause of her distress but were baffled – until the moment when we decided to leave and she began bellowing loudly again. Like most babies, she did not approve of being left on her own and was insisting that someone stay with her. Renee volunteered to remain with her for a while until Iris calmed down, but as soon as she tried to sneak out to go back to bed, Iris again started up her awful racket. Knowing that it would be impossible for anyone to sleep through the noise, Renee moved a camp bed into Iris's stable; this delighted the elephant, who promptly dozed off while Renee herself spent a sleepless night being kept awake by the contented snores of the baby elephant.

Renee spent the next week bedding down with her new charge but the sleepless nights were taking their toll. In the end we hit on the idea which human parents use; we provided Iris with a nightlight and although she bellowed angrily when she found her bedfellow was missing, she eventually settled down.

But that first week when they spent the nights together was something that Iris, like the proverbial elephant, 'never forgot'. The bond forged between her and Renee during that week was so strong that she would follow Renee all round the zoo, even into the house so that Renee could feed her a bottle of milk, which was later supplemented with balls of rice. Iris was amazingly gentle and well-behaved, and would spend hours playing with our Great Dane, Juno, curling her trunk round the dog's neck and leading her round the house, which looked extremely comical as at that time Juno was bigger than the elephant.

By the time she was eighteen months old Iris was a very large lady and had outgrown her cramped quarters and was ready to move into our purpose-built Elephant House – a project which had swallowed most of our money. So that she would not be lonely in her new home we decided to spend the rest of our dwindling resources on another elephant. After a long search we found a female Indian elephant of the same age as Iris, called Gitara, who was very placid; fortunately, the two elephants soon bonded and got on well together.

They would lumber around their enclosure, entertaining visitors and themselves by running in and out of their concrete bath while their keeper darted after them, scrubbing them with a broom. That particular keeper had worked with circus elephants, and with our blessing taught Iris some tricks. Within months she was persuaded to ring a hand bell with her trunk to signal to zoo visitors that her performance was about to start.

Once an audience had gathered, she would go through her repertoire, playing a giant mouth-organ and simultaneously dancing to the tune. On command she would roll over and 'Die for the Queen', would stand and lift her feet on to a plinth and thoroughly enjoyed every minute of being the centre of attraction.

It wasn't all plain sailing, naturally. We had tried to make the elephant enclosure as open-plan as possible and the only thing which separated the elephants from the crowds was a deep concrete ditch. The only problem was, the elephants seemed to be attracted by the ditch and Iris in particular liked to play by the edge, teetering on the brink like a tightrope walker, until one day she lost her balance and fell in.

She was terrified and so were we, because she was completely wedged in the ditch unable to move as we ran to fetch ropes and bales of straw and enlisted the help of the keepers to prop her up and drag her out. It was hazardous for us and stressful for Iris and it taught us a big lesson. The unfenced ditch might be far more aesthetically pleasing to the public but it was too dangerous for the animals. Still determined to retain an open-plan enclosure if at all possible, we resorted to erecting an electric fence along the edge of the ditch, but we had reckoned without Gitara, who had always been somewhat of a vandal and took great delight in wrecking things. The electric fence was no exception. She soon discovered that it was worth putting up with a slight shock to short-circuit the current when she could take her time dismantling it completely. In the end we had to give in to the inevitable and had a strong metal rail erected to prevent any more catastrophes.

Another memorable incident was the day Iris escaped. Workmen had been hired to freshen up the paint in the Elephant House and one of them had carelessly left one of the outer rails down. Ever the opportunist, Iris simply walked out.

When I arrived I found her sitting on the bonnet of their van, her enormous bottom hanging over the edge while she tried to lift the body of the vehicle with her trunk. When she saw me, she left her new toy and ambled over to greet me and allowed the keeper and myself to lead her back into the House while the crestfallen decorators stood staring speechlessly at the front of their van, which was completely squashed.

Iris remained a favourite with zoo visitors for many years. Gitara's behaviour worsened; always an inveterate vandal, she became more destructive, turning her attention to the walls of the Elephant House, which she repeatedly headbutted. The climax came during Christmas week when one wall which she headbutted began to fall apart and we thought the whole building might collapse, leaving us with the impossible task of finding other heated accommodation before the elephants suffered from hypothermia. We wracked our brains to find a solution. In the end we decided that the kindest thing for Gitara was to let her go to another zoo where a change of scenery and the possibility of her being mated might help her quieten down. Belfast Zoo offered her a home and she went on breeding loan there.

It is always sad when we have to part with any animal, very hard for me and often harder for the keepers who are with them every day and build up close relationships, but always we have to put aside our own feelings and do what we feel is best for the individual animal and the others at the zoo.

As Gitara was loaded on to the transporter that would take her to Belfast, I consoled myself with the thought that she would be well looked after and would have the chance of mating and having her own calf. The last sight I had of Gitara was of her holding a wadge of hay in her trunk and waving it to us as the transporter pulled away.

The summer of 1970 was glorious, with hot, languid days when all the animals were out basking in their enclosures. It was also a time when we were dealt a bitter blow. Our curator, Renee Carley, was taken ill and after an exploratory operation, doctors at the hospital broke the news to us that she was terminally ill with lung cancer, and had only a few months to live.

Renee herself never mentioned her illness. Pale and drawn, she insisted on coming back to work, saying she was perfectly fit. We knew that the place she would want to spend most time in was the zoo, in the company of the animals she loved, and could only accept her wishes with the same grace she showed in accepting that she had cancer.

It was hard to stand back and watch her as she struggled to do her job and pretend there was nothing wrong. We decided that the one thing we could do was to take on a deputy curator to help with her duties and we appointed John Voce, formerly of Coventry Zoo, to the position.

At least he could take some of the pressure of work off her without making her feel that we no longer felt that she was capable. Even so, it was heartbreaking to see her carrying on through the bitter winter months. Although she was looking tired and desperately ill, she insisted on hand-rearing the baby animals she loved. Until a week before her death she was still keeping a tiny baby gibbon in her room and sitting up all night to feed it.

Renee was one of those exceptional people who knew just by looking at an animal that it was ailing. When she died in May 1971 the tiny gibbon that she had so lovingly hand-reared was out in a run, and many of the animals who owed their lives to her were playing in the spring sunshine; constant reminders of the loyalty she had shown to the animals and ourselves over the years.

We planted a magnolia tree outside the house in her memory and every time I pass by, it brings back memories of Renee and the animals she loved. Whenever we take on a new keeper I look for the same instinctive sensitivity and rapport that she had with the animals.

Life must go on and the decision to part with Gitara meant that we would have to find a replacement elephant or elephants for Iris. It had always been our ambition to breed our own baby elephants and with this in mind we decided to look for two young female elephants. It was not just a selfish decision. There are fewer than 30,000 Asian elephants left in the wild, which is why the Asian Captive Elephant Breeding Programme is extremely important to ensure the survival of the species.

Before embarking on a search for two new elephants we agreed that this was the ideal time to submit plans to build a new, specially designed Elephant House to replace the old breeze-blocked structure. We were determined that the new Elephant House would be constructed to withstand any headbutting inhabitant and would afford its large occupants a more pleasing environment. We selected an undeveloped area at the far end of the zoo beside the Giraffe House, where we would have room to expand should we be lucky enough to breed more elephants.

The overall size of the new Elephant House we had designed was enormous, large enough for big trucks and JCBs to drive in, and it took a staggering six months to lay the foundations and nearly another six months to finish the building and landscape the half-acre enclosure.

The building comprised of double walls, the outside of neat red brick; the interior walls, twenty-two feet high, were made of concrete, reinforced with steel bars up to twelve feet high. For safety, the enclosure had a walled surround with a ten-feet-deep ditch, while the main enclosure where the elephants could roam freely had rocks embedded into concrete and a large pool so that they could bathe and have the mud wallow they loved and which was so good for their skins.

While all this work was in progress, we scoured other zoos and contacted dealers to see if we could locate two young females for our breeding programme. Locating the right animals was far from easy. In the end we heard that a dealer in Rotterdam had a whole collection of elephants for sale and we lost no time in arranging to see them. It was Christmas week and a bitterly cold December wind swept the airport when we arrived and drove by taxi to the dealer's premises on the outskirts of Rotterdam. Even with the heater full on I had never felt so cold and wondered how on earth young elephants just over from the Tropics could cope with these sub-zero temperatures. That question was answered when we arrived at our destination to find an enormous heated tent erected in a field. A giant marquee, it housed elephants of all shapes and sizes, from fully-grown bulls and cows down to smaller young calves. It was a totally surreal scene to see creatures that would naturally be living on the plains of Africa or in the jungles of India being paraded up and down before us inside a heated canvas cocoon in the middle of a frozen field.

We did not have to look any further than the two smallest females, who were just six years old; we fell in love with them immediately. Their names were Minbu and Tonzi and they had been bred and brought up in a logging camp in Burma, with the identifying stars tattooed on their rumps to prove it. They had been with humans all their lives, which meant they were very sociable and would fit happily into life in the zoo. The asking price was £6,000 each and it cost another £3,500 to have them transported over to England.

Meanwhile, Iris had now been moved from her battered old Elephant House into the new, more suitable building.

She had relished the pool and the mud wallow, delighting in hosing herself and her two keepers down.

Minbu and Tonzi travelled extremely well and settled into their new home together almost immediately. Although they were both friendly, Minbu was the more reserved of the two while Tonzi was more mischievous and outgoing.

Iris accepted the two younger elephants quite readily. Although she had related more to people than to Gitara, she was obviously glad of their company and would follow them around the enclosure and play in the water with them. Sadly, their friendship was shortlived. Iris developed a foot problem and although it was just a routine treatment, she had to be given an anaesthetic to put her out. Everything went smoothly and Iris came round from the anaesthetic only to have a fatal heart attack.

The only thing we were thankful for was that although the two young elephants missed their older companion, at least they had each other for company.

Six years later when Minbu and Tonzi were twelve years old they had reached the ideal age when they could be mated. Back in the logging camp they would have been turned out into the wild to find their own bull elephant with whom to mate; in captivity the breeding of elephants is strictly and scientifically controlled under the auspices of the Asian Captive Elephant Breeding Programme.

It is the ambition of most zoos to breed an elephant, but the whole process from mating and conception is carefully monitored. The females are genetically matched to a suitable bull elephant in order to produce strong, healthy offspring.

In the case of our two ladies, Chester Zoo kindly suggested we use their young bull elephant, Chang, who had an excellent track record. Knowing how experienced their keepers were in these matters, we had every confidence in entrusting the well-being of Minbu and Tonzi to their care. Even so, the gestation period is a nerve-wracking twenty-two months, a time when even the most careful planning can go wrong.

They would need to be mated at the time of ovulation in the middle of their oestral cycle, which in the case of female elephants is roughly every three and a half months. We catalogued these religiously and took regular urine samples over a period of twelve months, as timing was crucial if they were to successfully mate with the bull elephant and conceive.

When the day came for our two heavy cows to leave for Chester, Tonzi was already in season and Minbu due to come into season within three weeks. Always amenable, Minbu and Tonzi were extremely well-behaved and made no fuss about being loaded into the long transporter we had hired to make the four-hour journey; they arrived unstressed and unscathed at their destination. Now we just prayed that our calculations were correct.

The introduction of Minbu and Tonzi to their prospective mate was achieved over a period of two days when they were put into an enclosure alongside the bull elephant's quarters so that they could become accustomed to each other. On the second day Tonzi was mated and three weeks later Minbu followed suit.

We were jubilant and expected, if all went well, to have them back within three months, but it was not to be. An adviser to Chester Zoo, someone who had studied rhinos in Africa and who had been scanning the females, had informed them that unless the foetus had reached a fairly advanced stage and was properly formed, moving the mother could cause her to abort or re-absorb the unborn infant.

Chester Zoo were marvellous in agreeing to keep our females until it was safe for them to be transported home. We greeted the decision with relief, knowing that Minbu and Tonzi would have the best possible care, and yet we felt frustrated at not having our elephants back with us for twelve months.

CHAPTER ELEVEN

Light of the World by Jumbo Jet

We were not despondent for long. A call came from Jaldapara Wildlife Sanctuary, a National Park situated in West Bengal, where the elephants are used to take tourists to see rhinos and other wildlife in their natural habitat, asking if we would like to give a home to a two-year-old female elephant in return for supplying a pair of zebras and two chimps to Calcutta Zoo. This kind of exchange is a typical example of the worldwide co-operation which is common these days amongst international zoos.

The elephant they were offering was called Noor-Jahan, which means Light of the World. She had been born in a village on the National Park and had lived all her life wandering freely around the village surrounded by children and adult humans.

At night she was tethered to a tree on the edge of the forest for safety, and if it had not been for her exceptional good nature which endeared her to everyone, and the fact that the sanctuary wanted to restock with chimps and zebras, she would probably have followed in her ancestors' footsteps ferrying tourists around the park. But the officials at the sanctuary felt that out of all the elephants, Noor-Jahan would most readily adapt to zoo life and would be ideal to eventually breed from.

As far as we were concerned, when we were offered Noor-Jahan it seemed like perfect timing. Her arrival would almost coincide with Minbu and Tonzi's return from Chester, which would give them time to get to know each other before the birth of the two calves. With luck, the young elephant could become aunt to the new arrivals, bridging the gap between them and their mothers' generations.

We knew there would be many obstacles before we could transport Noor-Jahan to Britain, not least acquiring the zebras and chimps to give in exchange to Calcutta Zoo. We had to locate zoos which did have surplus stock and persuade them to trade with us. In the end we found a pair of zebras in a zoo in Israel and two chimps from another zoo which was finding it difficult to keep them. That problem overcome, we then had to arrange transportation for Noor-Jahan from her home in Jaldapara to undertake a two-day journey to a quarantine centre close to Delhi. There she would have to spend a compulsory four weeks, during which time she would be vetted to make sure that she was not carrying any diseases including foot and mouth disease, which would bar her from entry into this country.

In order to do this we would have to pay a vet to go over and carry out the necessary tests, and also dispatch experienced elephant-keepers who would supervise the journey and spend the month at the quarantine camp with Noor-Jahan.

We tentatively asked Roger Coley, the zoo's veterinary surgeon and our friend for many years, if he would like to go out for an all-expenses-paid holiday to India and take on the responsibility of carrying out the required tests on Noor-Jahan. To our great relief he readily agreed.

The other members of the team who would supervise transportation and the elephant's welfare were John Ray, our Zoo Manager, and Neil Williams, one of our experienced elephant-keepers. We were also lucky enough to enlist the help of Chris Webster from Woburn, who had first-hand experience of transporting elephants from overseas.

After extensive consultation with the officials at Jaldapara Wildlife Sanctuary, the complicated operation was planned down to the latest detail. Roger Coley, Neil Williams and Chris flew to Calcutta and then set off on the four-day journey by road to West Bengal for their first encounter with Noor-Jahan.

The journey was exhausting. Relentless heat, arid dusty roads and constant attacks from insects turned the days into a nightmare for the three men. Only the thought of 'The Light of the World', Noor-Jahan herself, kept up their spirits.

They were not disappointed. On arrival at the village where she lived they were introduced to the charming elephant, who stood around five feet six inches tall and weighed three-quarters of a ton and who accepted gifts of fruit from them before following them around like a cumbersome but friendly dog.

It was Roger Coley's job to do the first set of blood tests to confirm that she did not have any diseases before she could make the two-day journey to the quarantine headquarters near Delhi, where she would spend another month and undergo another set of tests before being flown back to England.

Once those initial blood tests had come back negative, Roger was free to make his own leisurely way to the quarantine quarter near Delhi. Meanwhile Neil and Chris set off with Noor-Jahan inside a crate roped on to the back of a lorry for the quarantine quarters. Any misgivings they had were soon dispelled when Noor-Jahan walked calmly into the crate and appeared more interested in eating than in what was going on around her. Even when they had to make stops she made no fuss until they finally arrived two days later at their destination.

John Ray, our Zoo Manager, a tall, bearded, quietly-spoken Scot who had originally come to Twycross as our bird man before he became absorbed with elephants, was already in Nepal on holiday in Kathmandu indulging in his first love, birdwatching. He now joined Neil to act as companion and supervisor for Noor-Jahan for the next month. Roger Coley was already at the quarantine quarters to take samples to make sure that Noor-Jahan was not carrying foot and mouth disease or swine fever, complaints which are carried by elephants. Should any traces be detected, the elephant would not be allowed to come to England.

A long drench was inserted down Noor-Jahan's throat to scrape it for a sample for analysis. Ordinarily it would have been a difficult undertaking but, again, Noor-Jahan showed impeccable tolerance by allowing Roger to perform the procedure without demur. Again the tests came back negative and Roger left to take a well-earned holiday before flying back to England.

Meanwhile, John Ray was discovering that conditions at the quarantine were primitive to say the least. The area consisted of eight acres of grassland inhabited by snakes, mongooses, an assortment of monkeys and thousands of mosquitoes.

The vegetation was perfect for Noor-Jahan but the accommodation for John and Neil was nothing more than a chicken shed with brick walls to a height of three feet, topped with one-inch wire netting. The beds were wooden frames with plastic weaving strung across to form a bare uncomfortable mattress.

Neil, who had the advantage of arriving first, had already chosen the bed which had a reasonable mosquito net slung above it, but John had to settle for a flimsy mosquito net which had alarming holes in it. The two thin blankets barely kept out the cold as the temperature plummeted at night and he slept with all his clothes on for ten days in a vain attempt to keep warm and fend off mosquito attacks before managing to buy a new net. Even then he would wake at three in the morning to find hundreds of mosquitoes clinging to the net trying to get in. Not only were the two men sharing their bedroom with hundreds of marauding insects but they had their fair share of geckos – small lizards – who also invaded the room.

During their enforced stay both Neil and John lost two stones in weight while Noor-Jahan thrived and enjoyed every minute in her new surroundings. She was kept in a half-acre area surrounded by a wall, and every morning, much to her delight, a little man would arrive on a three-wheel bicycle with a carrying box on the front laden with freshly cut grass and sugar cane. The little man spoke no English but would depart happily with two rupees clutched in his gnome-like hand.

If the sleeping accommodation was primitive, the other facilities were non-existent. There were no loos and no hot water, so John and Neil had to resort to having a bath in water troughs which were six feet long, five feet wide and four feet deep. Noor-Jahan paid close attention to their ablutions and on several occasions caused amusement and consternation by trying to wedge her large body into the trough to join them.

The only diversions during this month of quarantine were the stream of visitors, amongst them the foreign correspondent from *The Times*, who arrived having travelled the twenty miles from Delhi asking to meet the elephant who had become quite a celebrity since her arrival. When Roger received the results of the tests on Noor-Jahan and was given the all-clear, he flew home, leaving the two men and the elephant to wait another two weeks to complete the stipulated time in quarantine.

It was just as well they did have time on their hands because the crate in which Noor-Jahan had travelled from Jaldapara, crudely made by local villagers, was far too flimsy to risk housing her in for a ten-hour plane journey. John and Neil set about making it safe – a far from easy task when they were stuck on the edge of a jungle with no tools and did not speak the language. John scoured the local markets and villages searching for wood, chains, bolts, screws and implements to carry out the vital renovations to the box. If sign language did not convey what he needed, he often had to resort to striding behind a counter or into the back of a shop to pick out the item he required while the irate shopkeeper shouted and cursed him in some unintelligible dialect.

Miraculously, with limited time and resources the crate was made good. Noor-Jahan, who had followed with great enjoyment the sawing and banging which went on, made daily inspections of its progress and was encouraged to take an even closer interest when it was finally completed. Both ends of the crate were open and her feed was placed inside so that she had to walk in to get it, and she soon became accustomed to this routine; she was happy to walk into the box and content to spend her time in there eating. Both men hoped that this would make things easier when the day came for her to travel to the airport and be loaded on to a plane.

The crate would take up almost a third of the cargo space on the aeroplane and the thought of an elephant weighing three-quarters of a ton becoming fractious in mid-air did not bear thinking about.

While these events were taking place in India, back at Twycross we had our own share of excitement. At Chester Zoo, Minbu and Tonzi had undergone scans and urine tests which showed that both of the unborn calves were perfectly formed and healthy and were sufficiently developed for the elephants to come home. A lot larger than when they left, they arrived in a transporter totally unruffled and settled back into the Elephant House and zoo routine as if they had never been away.

Meanwhile, Noor-Jahan had begun her journey to Twycross. Any worries John and Neil may have had were dispelled when she walked placidly into her box, which was loaded on to a lorry for the trip to the airport, where she was lifted on to the plane without incident and took off for England – travelling very appropriately in a Jumbo jet.

It had been arranged for Noor-Jahan to land at Stansted Airport but as there was no Ministry vet available there the flight had to be re-routed to Schipol Airport in Holland, where she was inspected by a vet. Then, after being fed, watered and rested she was flown to Manchester Airport where she was met by a quarantine van.

Transferring Noor-Jahan in her crate into the van with a forklift truck was no easy task, but Noor-Jahan, although showing great interest in the proceedings, was completely unperturbed throughout the operation.

Her flight companions, John Ray and Neil Williams, waited until she was safely loaded and then followed the van back to her new home at Twycross.

April sunshine greeted Noor-Jahan when she walked accommodatingly out of her crate and looked round curiously at her new surroundings. We watched the elephant raise her trunk to take in the smell of jonquils and freesias that lined the route towards the farm building which had been converted into temporary quarantine quarters and would be her home for the next few weeks. A Ministry vet arrived to check her over before a very tired but unperturbed elephant was fed, watered and bedded down.

Within days she had endeared herself to everyone and adjusted effortlessly from her former life in the primitive Bengal village to living in an English zoo. For Noor-Jahan it was like swapping one set of admirers for another.

When her quarantine was completed she began to take daily strolls around the zoo with John or Neil to get her accustomed to her new surroundings. As she took her daily walk she was steered in the direction of the elephant enclosure where Minbu and Tonzi were enjoying their morning games in the pool, squirting themselves with water. The two elephants paused in their ablutions to watch her pass by and walked alongside to take a closer look at the newcomer. Noor-Jahan took stock of these strange elephants but, presumably because she was so used to having other elephants around her, she was far more interested in the people who had come to see her.

After several days the next step to a closer introduction was to walk Noor-Jahan through the Elephant House while the other two elephants were in their indoor quarters. Even in this closer proximity the three elephants remained remarkably incurious and carried on with what they were doing.

When Noor-Jahan was taken into a section next to theirs some days later, although they squeaked at each other there was no over-reaction; if anything, Minbu and Tonzi kept their distance and tried to ignore their younger companion. This behaviour soon changed when Noor-Jahan was taken out for walks; then the two elephants gave up all pretence of indifference and would both pace up and down, fretting until she came back. We were now confident that they could be let out into the enclosure together with little fear that they would become aggressive and do her any harm.

In fact, possibly due to them being pregnant, Minbu and Tonzi took Noor-Jahan under their wing and showed strong maternal instinct by mothering the little elephant. They would lovingly caress her with their trunks and gently play with her, and she followed them devotedly. By the time Tonzi was due to give birth she and Minbu had totally bonded with Noor-Jahan but we wondered just how their relationship might change when they had their own calves.

We knew that the most critical time lay ahead for both pregnant elephants. In the wild, they would have lived in a family group headed by a Matriarch, usually one of the oldest female elephants, and would have already seen other elephants giving birth. They would have watched and learned how a mother cared for her calf, and would have played with the baby elephants, which would have prepared them for the experience of giving birth themselves. Our two elephants had none of this knowledge and no one could predict their reaction when Tonzi went into labour.

We had been given a sound piece of advice from a friend of ours, a former director of Basle Zoo. He had warned us that for many animals who start off as orphans and have not experienced being cared for naturally by their mother but have been brought up away from their natural family environment, giving birth could be incredibly traumatic. They might not understand what was happening to them and in many cases out of fear would kill the newborn baby, considering it some kind of alien.

He advised us to take precautionary measures to deal with any such reaction by giving the elephant a sedative – Strensil – so that she was too sleepy to harm the calf when it was born and would have time to get used to its presence. This warning added more anxiety to an already stressful time when everyone was on tenterhooks waiting for Tonzi to go into labour.

We had made endless preparations to ensure everything went smoothly, including installing closed-circuit television cameras which covered every inch of the Elephant House where the expectant mothers slept, so that they could be watched twenty-four hours a day on a monitor in a nearby caravan manned by John Ray and Neil, who did the nightshifts. The well-known saying 'The best laid schemes o' mice an' men gang oft a-gley' certainly applied on this occasion. The unforeseen happened when I slipped in the bathroom and fell heavily and was confined to bed when Tonzi went into labour at three o'clock one afternoon. How I fumed and fretted with frustration at not being able to watch the proceedings!

To add to the tension, Tonzi was in labour for an unnerving marathon of forty-two hours. Minbu, who was watching as she heaved and strained with each contraction, did not understand what was happening to her companion and was terrified. She kept trying to get to Tonzi to help but would then run away roaring her head off. The only creature present who was completely calm was Noor-Jahan; she had seen it all before.

All this was relayed to me by Nat, who would rush back to the house to give me the latest bulletin. The moment I had dreamed of had come and here I was stuck in bed and about to miss it. I was livid. Heaving myself up, I got dressed and, hanging on to the banisters, somehow managed to ease my way downstairs, but I was unable to make it to the Elephant House to see the birth of our first elephant.

For the safety of the keepers, Tonzi had been chained to stop her hurting them or the baby when it was born. Roger Coley, our vet, had arrived and joined the keepers who were on standby to give any assistance. A bale of hay had been placed alongside Tonzi to act as a barrier between her and the baby when it was born, and when she was in the final throes of labour it proved to have been a wise measure. The baby came into the world very quickly, literally popping out on to the floor, which frightened Tonzi who turned round and tried to kill the bale of hay instead of the calf.

While she was occupied with the bale, the keepers went in and dragged the calf out into an adjoining annexe and began rubbing it vigorously with towels and encouraging it to stand up. The vet meanwhile had given Tonzi an injection of Strensil to sedate her.

After two hours the baby was sufficiently recovered to be taken back to Tonzi and was placed alongside her. The keepers had made a braid harness for the baby in case there was any adverse reaction from Tonzi. This would enable them to pull the baby away quickly from its mother.

Still under the effects of the tranquilliser, Tonzi showed little reaction to her offspring as the keepers pushed the calf towards the teats, which are situated between the front legs of an elephant, to suckle.

Everyone held their breath as Tonzi allowed her calf to feed and showed her first sign of maternal instinct when Minbu came to get a closer look by pushing her away.

Tired but triumphant, Nat came back to the house to tell me all about it and we drank to the health of our newborn baby. We could not have been more delighted, for it was a female. She was only the fifth Asian elephant to be born successfully in this country.

Three weeks later when Minbu went into labour, all three

elephants were aware of what was about to happen and there was no trumpeting or tension, just an air of expectancy. The keepers followed the same procedure, but this time, when Minbu had been sedated and the baby taken away, it stood up more quickly and when it was returned to Minbu knew instinctively where to find the teats and began to suckle almost immediately. Again, to everyone's delight, this sturdy calf was female. It seemed too good to be true, an amazing event, and this time I *was* there.

It seemed fitting to ask the local Asian Community to choose our babies' names. They called Tonzi's daughter Tara, which means 'Star', and Minbu's baby Karishma, which means 'Miracle' – because she was.

Minbu and Tonzi were quite happy to share their offspring with Noor-Jahan, who took great interest in them, caressing them with her trunk and grooming them, fitting perfectly into the role of aunt as we had planned.

As the calves grew older, Noor-Jahan was allowed to look after them for brief periods which gave the mothers a welcome respite. The months passed and the babies became more adventurous; they would follow Noor-Jahan into the pool, where they splashed around in the water while Minbu and Tonzi kept a watchful eye on proceedings.

The success of our breeding programme created its own problems. With our elephant population more than doubled, we now had to think about extending the outside elephant paddock, which seemed simple but threw up its own jumbo setbacks.

We needed another ditched island with twelve-feet-high reinforced concrete walls, but this involved spanning two ditches. The structural engineers consulted with us and our manager John Ray, and we came up with the plan to build a bridge from the original elephant paddock to the other.

We gave the contractors the go-ahead to commence excavating a three-feet-wide, twelve-feet-deep ditch, which was filled with concrete reinforced with metal sheets to be left undisturbed to harden for ten days, after which the digger would dig the soil back from the inside with a suitable gradient to the bottom of the island.

What started as a simple idea became more complicated as the days rolled on. An area of land at each end of the island had to be left undug to allow heavy machinery to enter and exit. It sounded simple and looked easy on the drawing board, but in practice was a nightmare. The drainage from the bottom of the ditch of the first island was piped through to the bottom of the new ditch and continued down the centre to a large concrete tank. Next to it there was to be another tank for which a large hole had been dug, ready to receive it on an agreed date. The deadline came and went: no tank. We made a frantic phone call to the suppliers only to be told that it had not yet been made – but that we would receive it within the next three weeks! Meanwhile, the rain fell incessantly and the first tank filled up with water. To avoid disaster, the drainage from both islands had to be stopped to prevent flooding, which meant that our brand new ditch had two feet of water in the bottom, delaying the project even further.

When the new tank finally arrived it turned out not to be the one we were expecting but another we had ordered for the reed-bed filtration section. We were totally frustrated by this new delay but the contractors took it all in their stride; they decided that rather than waste any time they would take advantage of the delay to use their vast range of agricultural machinery – tractors, dumpers, diggers and a lowloader – to visit the local quarry to select three large pieces of rock ready to put into the centre of the new island.

They also used their time to stockpile the soil that had been excavated in heaps around the edge of the zoo grounds; they would eventually be landscaped, grassed over and planted with trees and shrubs, and in the autumn with daffodils and crocuses.

Non-stop heavy rain fell for another week, turning the

ground into a sea of red mud as the excavations filled up with water. We had aimed to have the project finished by Easter 2000 but reluctantly had to admit that this target was now impossible.

Over the years nothing changes; excitements, disappointments – we have learned to take them all in our stride. Work progresses inexorably, if slowly. Steel stanchions are put into place to form the bridge over the two ditches. The reed bed is dug out, lined, then filled with fine gravel and water, just waiting until there is no risk of further frosts before the reeds themselves are planted.

During the coming months there will be more landscaping to be completed, more pumps to be installed to take the water from the reed bed through the waterfowl pools and then re-circulate it back through the reed bed. A waterfall and stream will also be incorporated, which we hope will make it a conservation area, attracting wild birds and waterfowl including moor hens, mallard ducks and coots.

New fences have gone up and, now that spring is here, new grass is growing on the elephant island ready for the official opening later in the year.

As I write, the baby elephants, Tara and Karishma, are growing fast and like all youngsters have been learning to be obedient. This is an essential part of their schooling, so that they can be handled when necessary routine husbandry has to be carried out. Like us, they have to have their nails filed and it is essential that they learn to lift their legs when asked so that the soles of their feet can be inspected daily. They are also taught to raise their trunks and open their mouths so that their teeth can be inspected.

An elephant grows six complete sets of molars during its lifetime. The set consists of four molars, one each side of the upper jaw and one each side of the lower jaw. The surfaces of these are ridged so that when the elephant chews its food it moves the lower jaw backwards and forwards in a grinding action which, after a period of time results in the molars wearing down, at which point they are replaced by new teeth growing up behind, pushing the old ones out.

In the wild, by the time the elephant reaches old age and its sixth and last set wears down, making it difficult to chew, the animal gets less and less nourishment as it is unable to digest its food and can lose condition, become weak and die. Elephants also need regular skincare. In captivity this is done by providing a pool and an artificial mud wallow. They also have a regular washdown with a hose once a day.

The Asian elephants are the biggest animals in the zoo and are the biggest eaters, consuming enormous meals. In the wild they spend up to sixteen hours a day eating vast quantities of different grasses, barks and shrubs. Up to 150 kilos is consumed and less than half is digested. Even before the babies are fully grown, our five elephants get through five bales of hay, five buckets full of fruit and vegetables, carrots, apples, cabbages, bananas and potatoes, six loaves of bread, zoo nut concentrates, bran mash, brown wild rice, cod liver oil, molasses, Equivite and linseed cake, the whole of which is washed down with at least a hundred gallons of water every day.

The fact that they are thriving is a testament to their good diet and the care afforded to them by their dedicated keepers.

In the wild, elephants like ours have a *mahout* or keeper whose sole responsibility is the care and welfare of the animal. These mahouts will usually remain with one particular elephant for the whole of his lifetime, and are usually employed to take tourists on sightseeing tours or work with the elephants in logging camps, where the huge creatures are used to move timber and logs from the forest.

Asian Elephants are endangered, but thanks to breeding programmes in zoos like Twycross, we know that future generations will have the privilege of seeing them.

The African Elephant, the one with the bigger ears, is now under great threat since the recent partial lifting of the ban on ivory. This can only encourage poachers who kill them for their tusks and sell the carcass for bushmeat. Like all animals in their natural habitat, their lives are at risk from human predators.

There has been much debate about the desirability of keeping animals in zoos but, compared with the risks outlined above, those animals get regular veterinary attention, good food, heated quarters and their own personal attendants. Which would you prefer?

CHAPTER TWELVE

Orangs through our Window

It had been a dreadful sleepless night as I dozed fitfully on the edge of the bed, constantly aware of the large bedmate beside me and waiting for a big red hairy arm to flop across me yet again. I was hot and bothered and regretting every minute of having volunteered to act as Florence Nightingale to a sickly young male Sumatran Orang Utan called Toby.

In the past I had often shared my bed with sick chimps, who had shown their appreciation by *not* hogging all the space and occasionally snuggling up to me for a cuddle. So when we found Toby lying in the corner of his cage with a soaring temperature and realised he was much too ill to be left alone at night, I brought a camp bed into the lounge and slept with him for the next uncomfortable week.

As Toby's portly figure edged across to take up all of the bed, I had to cling to its edge. All night long he inconsiderately tossed and turned, cudgelling me with his hairy ginger arms, and each morning I staggered up feeling as though I had not slept at all, with the black circles under my eyes to prove it.

Only the memory of already having lost one of our female orangs, Jeannie, a year previously, strengthened my resolve to stick it out. Jeannie had also been found ill in her cage, vomiting continuously and with a slight bleeding from her nose. Our vet, Mary Brancker, was mystified but gave her a routine antibiotic injection.

We sat up all night with Jeannie until the vomiting

diminished but her condition deteriorated until she lapsed into a coma and within twenty-four hours of us finding her she was dead. A post-mortem revealed that she had suffered a brain haemorrhage; only then did a member of staff recall having seen her fall, hitting her head on the floor. Because she had not fallen any great distance, the keeper had ignored the incident.

After the chimps the orangs were, both financially and emotionally, the most valuable creatures in our growing collection. To lose one was devastating and I had no intention of letting Toby die, no matter how uncomfortable it was acting as his night nurse.

By the fifth night, when Toby's condition began to improve, I was so worn out that I fell into a deep sleep oblivious to the fact that my patient, feeling better, had climbed out of bed to explore. It was a noise from the other side of the room that startled me into wakefulness. Someone was rifling through the Welsh dresser. My first thought was that it was a burglar. I reached out and switched on the lamp beside the camp bed to see all the dresser's doors wide open, its contents strewn across the floor, with Toby sitting happily in the middle of the mess noisily crunching a bag of crisps.

I sighed with relief, not only because Toby had made a spectacular recovery but also because both he and I could now return to our own beds.

Jod and his ill-fated mate Jeannie were our first pair of Bornean Orang Utans and were later joined by Sumatran Toby and his mate Trudy. Jeannie's untimely death had dashed our plans to breed from both pairs, but now we had to postpone finding Jod another female until he was older and we could afford one. Meanwhile, as they were so young, they were happy to share their House and their outdoor playpen, and visitors would spend hours watching their antics.

Although the two species of orang are from similar origins, the physical differences are considerable. Orangs more than any other primates resemble human babies, as they are born with no hair on their faces and the few sparse wisps on their heads turn them into Stan Laurel lookalikes. As they grow older, the hair on their heads flattens and coarse facial hair begins to grow to match the untidy red body-hair, which has the texture of coconut matting.

Sumatran Orangs are much more upright than their cousins from Borneo and do not develop the cheek flanges of fat and tissue called 'Gular pouches' that the male Bornean acquires when he reaches sexual maturity.

Because they are two individual types, world zoos have a policy not to crossbreed, which would produce hybrids, but to breed true specimens of each kind – which is so important if the species is to be saved from extinction. When we moved to Twycross in 1963, baby orangs were still being illegally captured by shooting the mother; this accounts for the dramatic decrease in the world orang population, which has now plummeted to less than 5,000 in total. Natural hazards, like the fires which have swept the forests in Sumatra, have also taken their toll, wiping out endless orangs who died from burns and smoke inhalation. Loss of natural habitat as civilisation continues to encroach on the forests where they live is another factor that has decimated the orang population, which was why we felt it so important to play a part in breeding these amazing creatures.

Although I loved the orangs, I had never built up as close a relationship with them as I had with the chimps. They were older when they came to us and unless you have an animal as a baby you can never establish such a close bond. It was their keeper, Meg Muschamp, who joined us from Chester Zoo, who had Toby and Trudy living with her in the cottage which adjoined our house. She became a mother figure to them and had the same understanding and rapport with them that Nat and I had with the chimps, and it was a relief to have someone as dedicated, capable and knowledgeable as Meg who could take over the responsibility for these important animals.

We had always treated the orangs differently for several reasons. They differed from the chimps physically, being second in size to a gorilla, with an arm-spread in an adult male as great as 92 inches – nearly eight feet! Their bodies are heavier, their legs shorter and weaker, making them far less agile than their smaller cousins.

Their likes and dislikes also differ from those of the chimpanzees. They are fascinated by brightly coloured blankets and take inordinate delight in draping them over their heads, to the amusement of visitors. Over lunch Nat and I get endless pleasure from looking out of the window to the orang enclosure to see a familiar lumpy shape hidden under a pink blanket sitting at the top of one of the trees.

In the wild the orangs will collect branches and leaves and weave them together to make a nest or even to use as a makeshift umbrella to shelter under from the rain. Mentally they are much slower than the quick-witted chimps, and although they can learn to use a hammer, undo bolts and play with toys, they do it slowly; however, where a chimp is easily bored, an orang utan scores ten out of ten for perseverance.

As our three baby orangs grew into strong adolescents, Jod the elder was the first to sexually mature and achieve spectacular facial pouches. Two years later, when Toby also reached maturity, they had to be separated before they started to fight to establish dominance. During such fights they would be perfectly capable of inflicting terrible wounds or even killing each other. Jod was moved to an adjacent cage and Toby and Trudy stayed together – and to our delight, Trudy became pregnant.

We were very excited and took every precaution to ensure that the birth would go smoothly, removing Trudy to a separate cage from the males, who in the wild live a solitary existence. By contrast, female orangs live in a group and they would normally be in attendance observing the birth. Instead it was Meg who watched over Trudy like a mother hen, checking her constantly.

For once Trudy broke the pattern of our other animals,

most of whom gave birth in the middle of the night, by going into labour at 8.30 one morning. It was a thrilling time, for after shutting the outer doors to keep out the public, Meg and I were able to watch the birth through the window.

As the contractions came more frequently, Trudy, with all the assurance of a seasoned mother, walked over to one of the wall shelves and, holding on to the two wall brackets that supported it, braced herself against the wall and proceeded to push down. Ten minutes later she was rewarded by a small, bluish scrap of flesh which lay squirming on the floor. We were overjoyed but Trudy was horrified and, shrieking loudly, she pushed it violently away from her and ran over to the window as if imploring us to help.

After some minutes of this behaviour Meg and I decided that we had to risk going into the cage if the baby was to stand any chance of survival. With many orangs or other apes, such an action would have been impossible; we would have been instantly attacked, but Trudy was a very gentle orang and we had to take some kind of action. Gingerly Meg and I let ourselves into the cage and, without taking our eyes off Trudy, carefully picked up the baby to dry him off. At any moment we expected her maternal instinct to take over and for her to wrest him from us, but even when we tried to put the baby to her breast she turned her head away, a look of revulsion coming over her face as we tried to persuade the baby to feed by putting her nipple into his mouth. Neither he nor his mother responded. The only positive thing was that Trudy had enough confidence in us not to fight us off.

For the next fourteen hours we tried to persuade her to nurse her baby but made no progress. Her rejection was complete, and by now the little mite was beginning to look dehydrated and blue. We knew that his only chance of survival was if we hand-reared him and so we took yet another baby into the house.

At first Kaya Kaya was fed every two hours, day and

night, on special powdered milk containing all the necessary vitamins, which had to be flown over from Holland, until his condition was stable. We found that, just like human babies, he could survive quite happily with a feed at midnight and would sleep through until six in the morning. By the time he was six months old he was a thriving healthy young chap who was growing rapidly and had become quite established in the household.

Under normal circumstances, female orangs will only mate every four years when their infant is weaned, but because Trudy had not reared her baby she was ready to conceive again and became pregnant as soon as she resumed co-habiting with Toby. We looked forward to the birth of her next baby even though we were well aware that history might repeat itself. Sadly, we were right. Although the birth was straightforward and the baby strong and healthy, Trudy again rejected it, refusing to let it near her and screaming for it to be taken away. Again we had to rear the baby in the house. We named Trudy's second baby Lotus Blossom.

Trudy obviously had no recollection of being nursed by her own mother or of seeing babies being brought up at their mother's breast. Hers was a common enough reaction from animals that are orphaned. Occasionally they will have an in-built maternal instinct but more often, like Trudy, they do not understand what is required of them.

Even when she produced a third male offspring who weighed 6 lb, twice the weight of a normal orang baby, Trudy refused to accept him. This time, because of his size and determination, we left him with her, hoping he would overcome her dislike; instead, every time he attempted to reach her nipple, she retaliated violently and tried to kill him. Only our intervention saved Borg, as we called him, and we had no alternative but to bring yet another baby into the house. The babies now outnumbered us!

Most of our decisions at Twycross were born out of necessity and thus it was that with the safe rearing of our first orang baby we realised that the orang quarters in the stable-block were no longer adequate. We needed to have newly designed quarters that would safely house two 300-lb male orangs and a 150-lb female, with one infant and others to come.

No matter how meagre our finances, we *had* to treat this as a priority and somehow raise the cash. I was pondering this as I drove down one of the zoo's paths in my van at eight o'clock one morning, when, to my horror, I turned the corner towards the Orang House and saw that it was already too late. For a familiar red-haired figure was strolling nonchalantly towards me.

It was Jod – on the loose! Spotting me in the driver's seat, he headed straight for the van and I just had time to lock its doors before he reached the window, pressing his huge face against the glass just inches from my own and turning the door handle. When it refused to open he gave the door an angry thump, then his face disappeared from view as he bent down.

I soon found out the reason why when my side of the vehicle was lifted four feet off the ground, teetering alarmingly on its side before he dropped it with a mighty thump, bouncing me around. Because of Jod's enormous strength it was no effort to pick up the vehicle, and this was repeated several times as I sat petrified with fear that he would overturn it.

Then he was gone, his huge bent figure shambling towards the children's mechanical rides, which he proceeded to turn upside down before making his way to the nearby café, where he diverted his efforts to wrenching the drainpipes and guttering out of their sockets. There were screams from the café staff, who scattered, leaving just Nat, Meg and me to cope, and I thanked God that it was too early for any zoo visitors to arrive.

Deciding bribery was better than confrontation, I drove the van around to the café door and Nat dodged in to grab some sweets and began laying a trail of goodies to lure Jod back to his cage.

We called to attract his attention and threw a sweet in front of him. For a few moments it looked as though our plan had worked as he began to follow the tempting trail, but by the time he reached his third sweet he realised he had been having far more fun causing havoc and went back to the drainpipes, pulling them effortlessly down and tossing them aside like matchsticks.

We tried distracting him and talking to him, but it was to no avail. We could not ignore the fact that we were dealing with a dangerous wild animal who could turn violent if provoked. In the end Nathalie went back to the house to fetch our tranquilliser gun and with unerring accuracy fired the dart at her large hairy target. Seconds later Jod collapsed in an untidy heap looking like a hairy red hearth-rug. With help we lugged him unceremoniously into a wheelbarrow and trundled him back to his cage. When he came round he probably thought he had had a glorious dream, but for us it had been a total nightmare.

After that unnerving experience we lost no time in putting the building of a new, safer Orang House into operation, convincing our bank manager that our in-creasing number of visitors would bring in enough money to pay for it.

The design of the Orang House revolved around two considerations: to make it as environmentally friendly to the orangs as possible, and to have more built-in safety factors to eliminate any further attempts to escape. To achieve this, the manually operated sliding doors which, although heavy, were no match for the strength of an orang determined to push them open, were replaced with electrically operated doors closed by a compressor too strong even for a large ape to argue with. In addition we installed an alarm which would be activated if the door was left open.

The interior of the House consisted of two bedplaces leading off their day rooms, with reinforced glass down to the floor, glazed tiles from floor to ceiling and underfloor heating.

This open-plan design differed from that of the Gorilla House because, like many other monkeys, gorillas do not like being watched while they eat. Orangs are not at all phased by having an audience and will provide visitors with hours of amusement as they chew their food before retiring to one of the wall shelves to laboriously make a nest from the wood wool provided or envelop themselves in a blanket.

In addition to a dry ditch and a wall topped by armour-plated glass, we also added extra features to their outside enclosure to provide the exercise they needed. Like chimps and gorillas, orangs can walk, but because their arms are longer and their legs are relatively shorter and weaker in relation to their bodies, they walk quadru-pedally with their back feet clenched and their hands usually flat on the ground. They are incredibly strong, as demonstrated by Jod's ability to lift a car off the ground.

In the tropical rainforests of Sumatra or Borneo they live mainly high up in the trees, using their six-feet arm-span to travel agilely for miles, swinging from branch to branch. To enable them to exercise this ability, we decided to install three trees instead of the single tree in the gorilla enclosure.

We scoured the district to locate any oak trees that were being felled. Although other kinds of tree can be used, oak is the best because it does not rot so easily. One huge specimen eventually arrived under police escort – which again captured the imagination of the public, who turned up in droves to see our three trees 'planted' with the help of a ten-ton crane and several tons of cement which had been dropped into waiting holes.

Once the cement had set, the orangs were sedated, lifted on to wheelbarrows and wheeled in to take up residence in their new home. Our efforts were rewarded when they went out to explore their new enclosure and within minutes were sitting happily up in the trees.

CHAPTER THIRTEEN

The Sumatran Connection

Our breeding programme was given a boost when we were offered a female Bornean Orang as a mate for Jod. Someone with a sense of humour had called her Twiggy after Britain's popular sleek, skinny model. Our Twiggy's figure bore no resemblance to that of her namesake, for she looked more like a candidate for Weight Watchers. She was either grossly overweight or in the advanced stages of pregnancy, and we prayed it was the latter – being blissfully ignorant that she had rejected any previous babies she had produced.

Nor did we know that Twiggy was an accomplished vandal who would inspire our previously well-behaved orangs to copy her destructive ways. While the others were happily swinging around the branches or sitting in the crook of a tree, Twiggy, considering such activities too energetic, remained firmly on the ground. Instead she concentrated her attentions on digging up our carefully planted grass in the enclosure and proceeded to continue downwards until she unearthed some large stones. It was a slow and ponderous exercise but, with the perseverance unmatched by any of the other apes or monkeys, Twiggy achieved her goal.

Our first worry was that she intended to fling them over the armour-plated glass at any unsuspecting visitors, but Twiggy had other plans afoot. Carefully she carried the large stones into the indoor pen and began to attack our beautiful glazed tiles, cracking them until she could prise them off the wall so that she could reach the plaster and bite chunks out of it with her teeth. Fascinated by this new game, the other orangs soon joined in and, within hours, our ultra-luxury modern Orang House, the most prestigious building in the zoo, looked like a bombsite. We curtailed Twiggy's interest in the tiles by shutting her into an adjoining bedplace where she stayed for the remaining days until she gave birth. Away from her influence, Jod and the other orangs quickly forgot their tile attack and resumed their rightful place in the trees or swinging in their hammocks.

Without any fuss Twiggy gave birth to a small wrinkled baby which she allowed to cuddle up to her. Our relief was shortlived, however, as throughout the day, although she held the baby in her arms, we never saw it suckle. The nipples of an orang are situated under its arms and that is where Twiggy kept them, never lifting an arm up to give the baby any access, no matter how hard it tried. We decided to let her keep the baby in the hope that she would realise what she was doing wrong, and spent a thirty-six-hour vigil praying for the miracle to happen. By this time, the baby's condition was deteriorating and we had to make the decision to remove her. But that was not going to be easy. Unlike Trudy, even if she did not know how to look after her, Twiggy loved her baby and would not give it up easily.

In the end we gave Twiggy a drink spiked with a sedative, and only when she was in a deep, drugged sleep did we dare to creep in and take the baby from her.

By the time she woke up hours later, the baby had been given several nourishing feeds and looked more contented as she snuggled down in the arms of her surrogate mothers.

We had no idea what Twiggy's reaction would be when she found her baby missing. In fact it was very low key. Initially she searched her bedding and every corner of her room looking for it, and then became distracted by the special treats she was given and by the next day seemed to have forgotten she had ever had her baby.

A week later we returned her to the quarters she shared with Jod and within weeks she had mated and become pregnant again. This time we were determined that the baby should remain with her. We sought advice from other zoos and used Meg's considerable knowledge of orangs to formulate a plan. Providing the next baby was healthy, we would leave it with her for twenty-four hours. If by that time she was not feeding it we would put a tranquilliser in her drink and, when she was unconscious, go in and put the baby to her nipple and let Nature take its course.

The only thing we had not reckoned on was the baby itself, a bonny female in every way. When Twiggy was dead to the world and we placed her nipple in the baby's mouth, she refused to suckle. No matter how hard we tried she did not appear to have any natural instincts to feed. Still determined that the baby should stay with her mother, Meg volunteered to go in with mother and daughter to try and bottle-feed her.

This was not as simple as it sounds, because she knew it would be impossible to go in with a bottle for the baby without Twiggy grabbing it for herself. In the end she took them a bottle each and they both sucked happily away.

Our hopes that the baby might get hungry after its last 6 pm feed and begin to feed from her mother during the night were dashed. After six weeks we were no further forward and Twiggy had taken to wearing the baby on her wrist like a bracelet, swinging it up and down all day long. It was frightening to watch, as the baby became more and more distressed. In the end, we reluctantly had to admit defeat and take the baby away from her.

By now Twiggy had become aware that something was being put into her drinks and by sniffing at them suspiciously she managed to detect any which contained the drug and refused to drink it. Our only recourse was to use a tranquilliser dart to rescue the baby and so yet another orang was hand-reared.

Although many of our orangs did not make natural mothers and we ended up with a succession of babies in the house, we were able to fulfil the demands from other zoos for the offspring. It seemed that our orang breeding programme was at least helping to establish more of these lovely creatures, until one day we had a call from Chester Zoo. They had carried out a routine DNA test on a young orang we had supplied and discovered that it was a hybrid – half Sumatran and half Bornean.

We were devastated. The father could only have been Toby, and to our knowledge he had never been in close proximity with the Bornean female. Their quarters were adjacent but separated by heavy weldmesh, and it was only by observation that we realised that he had managed to mate with the female through the holes in the mesh!

We were mortified. It meant that all the orangs we had so happily sent away were hybrids and only suitable for exhibition, not for breeding, and we had to let the zoos in question know. It was highly embarrassing for us, but the recipients of our young orangs were very understanding and appreciated our honesty. The discovery of Toby's illicit matings prompted yet another adaptation to the Orang House, the fitting of armour-plated glass between the quarters of the two species of orang, which served to curtail his activities.

Over the years, most of our orang babies were reared in the house. Now our new keeper, Julie Dalley, is taking over the role of Mum to our latest rejected baby, Beau, whose natural mother, Gigit, following in what appears to be the tradition of most of our female orangs, promptly rejected him at birth.

Julie returned to the zoo two years ago after working with gorillas and Howler Monkeys, before taking over from Meg Muschamp when she retired.

Like many of the new generation of keepers, Julie is passionately interested in the animals she looks after and has struck up a tremendous rapport with them. To extend her knowledge, she and another keeper, Judith Seymour, applied to go as volunteers during their holidays to work in the Bohorok Orang Utan Rehabilitation Centre on the island of Sumatra. They wanted to see orangs in their natural habitat, feeling it would give them valuable knowledge and insight to help them with their charges at Twycross.

Their hopes were dashed when they were told that there were no more places available. Undeterred, they made enquiries and found a travel company which offered a package tour to Sumatra, including in the itinerary a four-day stopover at the Orang Rehabilitation Centre.

The rest of the trip was exciting, but for the two girls all the sightseeing paled in comparison with the chance to see orangs in their real setting. Situated in rainforests with mountains on one side, the station had been built twenty-five years ago by two Swiss zoologists from Frankfurt Zoo who set up the project under the umbrella of the Peneco Foundation in an area they considered ideal in which to release orangs into the wild.

The girls' first sight of the station and the rainforests was breathtaking, everything they had dreamed it would be. Both of them were awed when they saw orangs moving at speed in their natural habitat, surging effortlessly overhead through the trees. It was a thrill they would never forget, but other aspects of their visit were *not* so fulfilling. Pictures they had seen showed large areas of lush forests adjoining the Rehabilitation Centre. The reality was different. Over the years there had been tremendous deforestation, with logging camps clearing huge areas of trees. Also, with the influx of tourists to the orang centre with money to spend, a slum village had grown up close by. Both of these developments were bringing new dangers to the orang population. Many were being killed by swinging on the new overhead power cables erected as civilisation spread across the territory. Others were dying from viruses carried by the tourists and logging workers.

When the two girls introduced themselves to the centre's Indonesian curator, Mr Risnan Bangun, and explained that they worked at Twycross Zoo, he told them that if they had contacted him direct instead of applying to the Peneco

Foundation, he would have been delighted to give them work there for their three weeks' holiday.

He also explained that the Rehabilitation Centre was no longer an ideal halfway house from which to release semi-wild orangs into the neighbouring forests. The rehabilitation of the orangs had to be relocated to a new unspoilt area, with the present camp remaining as an educational and tourist centre. If this could not be achieved and the deforestation continued at its present rapid rate, he estimated the orangs would be extinct within six years. A sobering thought.

Armed with this information and an invitation to return the following year for three weeks to work as volunteers, Judith and Julie arrived back at Twycross with a mission – to help save the Sumatran Orangs. I did not need any convincing and lost no time in launching an Orang Appeal to collect public donations to help fund the valuable work of the rehabilitation project.

Two weeks after they returned from Sumatra, a long-term volunteer from Bohorok, Andy Blair, came to visit the zoo. He met up with Julie and Judith and offered to help them when they visited the following year. Andy has since given talks at Twycross to raise money for the new quarantine quarters in Sumatra, and we are sponsoring him to continue with the valuable work he is doing as Consultant to plan, design and manage the new orang project near Medaan in Northern Sumatra Province. His other task was to evolve a way that tourism and environmental education could help to sustain and safeguard the feral orang population in the surroundings of the Bohorok Rehabilitation Centre.

A year later, when Julie and Judith returned to Bohorok, they renewed their acquaintanceship with Andy and spent three weeks learning just what problems the orangs on Sumatra are facing.

Heading for the Rehabilitation Centre in a truck, they were caught in a traffic jam caused by a landslide and found themselves surrounded by the local Indonesians who saw very few white visitors and pressed their faces against the windows to get a better look. Green eggs, a local delicacy, were thrust at them through the open flaps, together with dried fishes, which are part of the staple diet of the region.

The girls were struck by the poverty of the people in the area of the rainforests, a complete contrast to the lifestyle of the city-dwellers. The family vehicle for Mum, Dad and two children was a bicycle. Their first sight of a family going out stopped them in their tracks. Dad sat on the saddle pedalling, with Mum and the two kids perched on the crossbar, the family dog balanced on the handlebars and a Pig-Tailed Macaque clinging to the pillion.

It was indicative of the value the family put on the Macaque, which was trained to climb trees and bring down coconuts, that it shared their only mode of transport.

Like the rest of the volunteers, the two girls were responsible for finding their own accommodation in the nearby village. It was Andy Blair who told them where there was a room available, which turned out to be cheap but not so cheerful.

For fifty pence a night they shared a dingy room which had no hooks on which to hang their clothes. They had to leave them in their bags on the floor or put them on the bed. A bathroom next door housed a primitive shower and a toilet that was nothing but a hole in the floor with a pipe which drained away the sewerage.

The smell of urine invaded the place, and after a few days Julie realised that if they continued to stay there they would both fall ill. Another volunteer staying at the same place had had rats running across his legs as he lay in bed.

The girls were already suffering from mosquito bites. Hundreds of mosquitoes attacked them during the day as they worked with the orangs in the forest. They could not even protect themselves from these dangerous insects by coating themselves with insecticide, because it might have a detrimental effect on the orangs, should any of the cream rub off and the animals put their hands in their mouths.

At night the insects invaded their room, biting them through the sheets. Judith in particular was badly affected, and she erupted in painful blisters which she had to bathe carefully. Even so, they formed nasty-looking scabs and when the two girls went out in shorts to visit an upmarket shopping centre, everyone stared at the sores on her legs and refused to get on the same escalator.

Deciding to push the boat out, the two girls moved from the sublime to the ridiculous. Their new hotel, The Jungle Inn, cost the princely sum of £2.50 per night! They were given the honeymoon suite, but it had no electricity. However, the view from the balcony of their room was amazing. It overlooked the river, where they could see the orangs when they came down out of the forest to drink.

Unfortunately, within days they were asked to leave because they did not spend enough money. Apparently the hotel not only had a restaurant but also organised treks into the jungle to see the wildlife, and as Julie and Judith never ate in the restaurant and were too busy at the Rehabilitation Centre to go on treks, the owners told them that unless they paid an increased tariff on the room, they would have to go.

Annoyed at being given an ultimatum, the two girls moved yet again, this time to a medium-priced lodging house where, for £1.50 per night, they got a room *and* electricity, although the current was so low that it took twenty minutes to boil a travel kettle and twenty-four hours to charge up the batteries on their camcorder.

During the three weeks they spent at the Bohorok Centre, Judith and Julie saw at first hand how the orangs have suffered from humans. Despite being so endangered, the illegal trade in baby orangs still thrives as poachers continue to hunt and shoot adult females to take their offspring to sell as pets.

And as Julie and Judith discovered to their horror, no one enforces the law and in many instances the very people who are supposed to protect the orangs – the

'Avez-vous a cuppa?' (By kind permission of the Brooke Bond Tea Company)

Clean bowled.

Proud moment. Sue with son Brooke, first chimp born at
Twycross Zoo. (John Doidge)

Molly with Flynn as a baby – the close bond still remains.
(*Leicester Mercury*)

Rosie the artist at work. Could this be another Picasso?
(John Drysdale)

Joe and Bongo as babies. (John Doidge)

Molly with a new orang baby. (News Team International)

Sue the chimp takes her turn bottle feeding our first orang baby. (John Doidge)

Our unusual trio. Gorilla baby Asante, Becky the chimp and Leelah the orang. (John Doidge)

Totty the otter investigates the plumbing. (John Doidge)

Baby Brazilian tapir. They don't come more appealing.
(News Team International)

One-week-old baby giraffe Keisha with mother Kaya. (Karen Miller)

Asian lions Khari and Bellamy – part of the European breeding programme. (Karen Miller)

Thirtieth anniversary of Twycross. Johnny Morris with Joli.

The house and gardens at Twycross in the spring.
(Karen Miller)

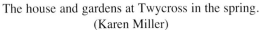

Forestry officials – are those responsible for supplying these babies to anyone willing to pay a good price.

In Medaan alone there are hundreds of orangs taken from the wild living as family pets. But as with the pet monkeys and chimps that were so popular with the British in the 1940s, when the cute baby orangs grow bigger and maturer, they are no longer wanted.

It is these orangs who desperately need the help of the Bohorok Centre. Having spent years in domesticity, they would never be able to survive in the wild. They have no idea how to forage for food or in some cases even how to swing through the trees. They are so used to humans that they have no fear of them and will approach villages to find food rather than live in their natural habitat in the forests.

It is then they discover that the humans they have learned to trust present the biggest threat to their lives, and will shoot to kill to keep them away from their property.

The younger the orang is when he comes to the Rehabilitation Centre, the better chance he has of learning to fend for himself in the wild. Far more tragic are the older ones who have only known human company and have never had to fend for themselves. One of these was a sixteen-year-old orang called Amok, who had been chained by a metal collar round his neck. When Julie and Judith first saw him they could not believe their eyes as one of the rangers came up behind Amok and lifted him off the ground. All they could see of the ranger was his legs sticking out from under the red hairy body. It was quite unnerving to watch, but the orang had been so used to humans that he accepted it as a bit of fun.

Teaching Amok to survive in the wild was extremely difficult. When he arrived at the Centre he had no idea how to climb or swing from branch to branch. Nor did he know how to make a nest for himself. All of these skills had to be taught by the rangers.

When they felt that it was time for him to try living in the forest they released him close to the Centre. Unfortunately,

Amok's early days were so imprinted on him that instead of foraging for food in the forest he constantly made his way to the rangers' houses or to the village, where he made a nuisance of himself and risked being shot.

The rangers were faced with two alternatives: to take Amok right away from civilisation and leave him to survive as best he could, or to have him put down. In the end they paired him up with another female who was due to be released and took them to one of the furthest points in the forest close to the mountains. They knew that on his own it was unlikely that Amok would be able to fend for himself, but with a companion who was far more skilled in searching for food and surviving in the wild he might be able to lead a more natural life. It was a risk they had to take. So far there has been no news or sightings of the two orangs.

Another unusual orang at the centre was a female who suffered from Down's syndrome, a condition which is rare in the species: it is even rarer that she survived. She had never learned to climb but had a very sweet, loving nature and she had found her niche at the Centre by acting as surrogate mother to some of the younger orangs. At night she would put her arms around three or four of the youngsters and cuddle them and they would all happily settle down with her.

Julie and Judith certainly found their visit enriching, but were also quite surprised at the basic lack of knowledge of the helpers in some areas of orang care. Hygiene left a lot to be desired and it was Judith and Julie who spread the word that utensils should be disinfected to avoid passing on infections.

They also watched in amazement as the rangers cracked raw eggs for the orangs when they knew that the animals were perfectly capable of doing it themselves. Another bone of contention, which reminded me of our past mistakes, was that the volunteers insisted that the orangs could not be taken out in the rain. As it rained every afternoon, it meant that the orangs were kept indoors. When Julie and Judith insisted on taking their charges out and playing with them in the warm humid rain, they found it was not a popular move as it meant that the other keepers had to follow suit and could not have an afternoon off.

Another point which worried our two keepers was the fact that none of the orangs were checked before they were released to see if they were carrying any disease. As Julie rightly pointed out, many of the orangs who had been in contact with humans had developed viruses and colds. One group had even caught chickenpox from visiting tourists. Although it did not prove fatal, they were all ill for a week. Had any one of these come into contact with orangs in the wild, in particular a female with a baby, they could have passed it on and the baby would not have survived.

This year, Julie and Judith will once more make their pilgrimage to the Bohorok Rehabilitation Centre, taking with them a cheque from Twycross Zoo. We are only too aware that the situation of the orangs in Sumatra is grave, and that they need all the help we can give.

Andy Blair has told us that one item which is desperately needed is a large Socialisation Cage in which orangs can get to know each other. This will cost £5,000 and we are hoping that by the time Julie and Judith go to Sumatra again, we will have raised this amount as our contribution to the valuable work that is being carried out to ensure that orangs on the island will survive.

CHAPTER FOURTEEN

Gorillas in our Midst

I knew the honeymoon with Joe, our first baby gorilla, was over the day he rushed across the room as we were watching a riveting programme on television, picked up the set and smashed it to the floor. Sparks flew and blue lights flashed angrily as it disintegrated in front of my eyes while Joe danced with delight. I thanked God that this was his last day in the house, an emotion I would never have dreamed I would feel.

When I first heard that a gorilla was available for us, I was very excited. A gorilla was the only member of the ape family missing from our collection at Twycross – and it was the one we coveted most.

I had been persuaded to do a promotional tour in Ireland and was away when the news came that there was a young gorilla for sale. I had mixed emotions when Nat told me all about it over the telephone that night. Of course I was excited – it was brilliant news! – but I desperately wanted to be back at Twycross when he arrived.

Instead I had to make do with daily bulletins from Nat, who explained that he was an eighteen-month-old male called Joe, who would cost us £600. In 1965 that represented a lot of money – but we would have sold every stick of furniture to have him.

We decided to keep him in as close contact with us as possible, in a cage in the house. And so it was that Joe the gorilla joined the long procession of baby apes who had come to live with us over the years. A strong cage was made for him and installed on the landing ready for his arrival, and I made constant telephone calls from Ireland to hear all the news until Nat said those magic words: 'He's arrived.'

Unlike our chimps, who took exception to being put in cages, our new gorilla went into his quite docilely and displayed a very amiable nature. I couldn't wait to finish the tour and get home to meet him. Nat told me that he was a sturdy little fellow who had immediately won the hearts of everyone.

The moment I set eyes on Joe I was entranced, for he was a magnificent specimen with black hair, shiny eyes and a disarming expression. Yet it wasn't all plain sailing. We soon learned to our cost that gorillas behave themselves very differently from chimps and orangs. In the wild, for instance, gorillas crash through dense jungle knocking down any obstacle that gets in their way – even uprooting small trees. Young though he was, Joe's behaviour was imprinted on him and he knocked down anything in the house which stood in his way – this included chairs, tables, anything really that caught his attention. He was a born wrecker.

This behaviour underlined for us the difference between the species. Chimps are eager to learn, and are very careful with their toys or delicate objects and will accept a slap as a reprimand if they are naughty. Gorillas do not respond to authority; they have a different temperament and ability, so Joe would crash through the house as though he was in the jungle, sending everything flying.

We soon delegated all our ornaments, those that he had not already destroyed, to high shelves which he could not reach as he did not have the same climbing ability as our chimps to get at them.

Even at his tender age he was far more powerful than any chimp or orang and far more boisterous. When he discovered that our Great Dane, Prince, would be only too happy to become his playmate, the two of them rampaged around the house chasing each other. Joe even allowed us to put a collar and lead on him so that we could take him for walks around the zoo with Prince. They were an unlikely couple but thoroughly enjoyed each other's company.

They would also go for drives in the car, with Prince lying flat out on the back seat and Joe gazing out of the window.

The highlight of Joe's day was his early morning bath. As soon as he was let out of his cage he would dive into the bathroom, and straight into the waiting bath – throwing up a huge wave of foam as he did so and splashing water everywhere! The bathroom was always awash, the towels soaking, and we often ended up being drenched, too.

The one worry we had as far as Joe's health was concerned was the diarrhoea which began two weeks after his arrival. The cause was finally tracked down to some kind of milk allergy, because we discovered that when he was given tea without milk he was fine. This was bad news, as Joe needed to consume pints of milk every day, along with loads of fruit, to provide him with all the calcium and protein a gorilla of his age required. Apart from this problem he was the picture of health, so we were not unduly concerned, but we did try just about every kind of milk, from baby milk preparations to goats' milk and soya – none of which made any difference. His allergy certainly did not affect his energy levels and he continued to blunder around the house causing mayhem on a grand scale.

Joe was now getting too rough to play with Prince, and that summer before we left for a holiday in Europe, Nat and I decided it would be a good idea to get him a companion of his own kind.

We found Bongo at a dealer's in Holland. She wasn't a magnificent specimen like Joe but a waif-like animal, tiny for her eight months and with little hair. Because she was quite frail, Mr and Mrs De Souza, the dealer and his wife, had taken her into their home and she had been brought up with their young baby. When we saw her she had a bad cold which would have put off most buyers, but even after all these years we still let our hearts rule our heads and agreed to pay £1,500 to take her when she was well enough to travel. Even if she had not had the best start in life healthwise, we felt that we would be very lucky to find another female gorilla that had been hand-reared and brought up with an infant.

By now, restrictions had been set in place and permission had to be granted before anyone could import any of the great apes; it took two weeks to apply and be given the necessary licence to bring Bongo into the country. Mrs De Souza impressed us with her concern by refusing to let the baby gorilla travel on her own. She flew into Heathrow with her charge, who came equipped with sets of baby clothes, nappies, special tins of milk diet and rusks. Bongo was very sweet and we made a great fuss of her before setting off for Twycross, looking forward to her first meeting with Joe.

After all our past experience with Mickey and Sue I don't know how we could have been so naïve as to think that Joe would greet Bongo with open arms. It was like history repeating itself. When Joe first clapped eyes on Bongo it was hate at first sight. He bared his teeth, leapt forward and dealt her a hefty blow, which bowled her over and left her howling. There was no way that any gorilla the size of Bongo could compete with one as powerful and aggressive as Joe.

All our best-laid plans for them to share a cage went out of the window and we spent the next few hours organising a new cage for Bongo which was installed in the office downstairs to give both animals breathing space. Having been on her own all her young life, Bongo was quite happy to stay there and Joe, having established his male superiority, returned to his rightful place upstairs.

Like all babies they needed a lot of attention and suffered the usual infant complaints, upset tummies, sore gums while teething, and running temperatures which made them fractious. Both wore nappies and had hug rugs. Joe used to play around the house and slowly and carefully we reintroduced them. Now that Joe had established his position as the leader, they would play together for a while, but we always had to have someone present to intervene if he got too rough.

We had hoped that Bongo would be able to join him at bathtime, but we were in for another surprise. Joe, it seemed, was more than happy to share his bath with her, but Bongo shrank away from the foamy water and hid herself in the furthest corner of the bathroom, wincing whenever he splashed any water near her. She could never be persuaded to get into a bath and just hated getting wet.

As time went on it became obvious that Joe and Bongo would never become the bosom buddies we had hoped for. In their own way they were still loners and we decided that it might help them to learn to socialise if they had companions of their own.

The only suitable animals we had at the time were chimps, and we chose Tina and Soco to take part in the experiment. Soco, the bigger chimp, we paired off with Joe, as she was quite able to take care of herself, and the other chimp, Tina, who was very clever but far more gentle, we felt would fit in with Bongo.

People thought we were taking a risk, because the gorillas were so much more powerful and aggressive than the chimps, but we knew our animals and were aware that, mentally, the chimps could run rings around the two gorillas; their greater agility and ability to climb would always keep them out of trouble.

On the whole our experiment worked well and the four lived amicably together, although the differences between the two species became more apparent. Tina and Soco played happily with toys and would spend hours learning new skills. Often the gorillas would take an initial interest but within minutes would get bored and would knock whatever the chimps were playing with out of the way, much to their annoyance. Although gorillas *are* intelligent, their attention span is short and they cannot concentrate in the same way that chimps and orangs can. Their sole aim in life seemed to be to smash as many things as possible in the shortest possible time.

When Joe was older we built outdoor cages with runs which had all kinds of interesting diversions, like ropes to swing on, suspended tyres, climbing frames and footballs, which gave our two gorillas the opportunity for much-needed exercise. Each night they came back worn out into the house to sleep, and all four seemed very contented with the arrangement.

If the weather was fine we would take the chimps and gorillas for walks around the zoo – much to the delight of any children they met on the way. The animals liked the attention and behaved impeccably with our young visitors, but with Joe's increasing size we knew that within a short time we would not be able to cope. Already he was aware that he was much stronger than we were and began to test how far he could go.

At night, he naughtily refused to go upstairs to bed and, knowing that he would win any test of strength, we wracked our brains to come up with a solution to outwit him. Suddenly remembering that he had always been very wary of our old tabby, we carried the cat to the stairs. One look and Joe bolted upstairs and shot into his cage.

This was repeated several times until Joe decided that the cat was just a stooge. From then on we were saddled with finding new objects with which to frighten him. Sometimes one of us would rather meanly jump out on him from the back stairs; more outlandish objects and animals were used to make him run upstairs.

It was a game in which he agreed to take part providing we abided by his unwritten rules. If we produced some pathetic object like a doll, he would stand his ground and look us in the eye and not budge until we had produced something which he would consider could conceivably 'terrify' him into pounding upstairs and into his cage. Rabbits, rats, monstrously large cuddly toys he would accept, but we knew that we were rapidly running out of ideas and time.

By now Joe weighed 100 lb, well beyond the stage of being physically manageable. Whatever our financial straits, we *had* to build a purpose-built Gorilla House for him and Bongo before they reached maturity. An adult male gorilla can weigh up to 400 lb and because of its very size has to be treated with respect. All animals are dangerous, and although when they are hand-reared they form a bond with those that have cared for them, when you enter their enclosure you are invading their territory and they can be unpredictable.

No matter how bonded Joe and Bongo had become with us, it was impossible to keep adult gorillas in a normal household.

Before undertaking the expense and upheaval of building a Gorilla House, we wanted to make sure that we had the best and most modern design, incorporating an outside area that was environmentally suited to the gorillas' needs and interior quarters with underfloor heating, colour television and lots of climbing apparatus to curb their energy.

By now, most zoos were getting rid of the old-fashioned bars and wire, replacing them with twelve-feet-high armour-plated glass panels which took away the feeling that the animals were captive and allowed them and the public an open-plan view. Frankfurt Zoo was one of the pioneers of this design and we wrote to them asking their advice, only to discover that the glass panels alone would cost £25,000 – twice the amount we had to spend on the whole Gorilla House!

We then tried writing to American zoos for their advice. Currently the vogue was to surround the enclosures with a wide, water-filled ditch, but feedback from those zoos that had adopted the method revealed that they had lost some animals who had drowned in the moat, so we dismissed that idea.

In the end we decided to take the two best ideas and

combine them. San Francisco Zoo used a deep *dry* ditch, and that, incorporated with a brick wall with five-feet-high armour-plated glass, should prevent the animals from reaching the ditch and the public from throwing things to the animals.

It also afforded both parties the best possible views so that the gorillas and the public could watch each other: it was debatable who entertained whom the most. Glass barriers, we discovered, had another benefit in that they also acted as a natural windbreak for our animals and, in the indoor quarters, kept the public and their germs away from our susceptible creatures.

The indoor layout consisted of two playrooms with their own sleeping quarters at the rear, where the gorillas could have the privacy they liked. It also meant that once they had decided to retire we could lock them in and the public would take this as a cue that the zoo was closing.

The walls of the House, like the orang quarters, were tiled from floor to ceiling and Joe had a sunken bath installed in his quarters so that he could still enjoy his bathtime splashabout. When a local company heard about the Gorilla House, they donated a colour television which was built into the wall so that Joe could not give a repeat performance of wrecking it. Ironically, the gorillas ended up with a much better set than our own!

To make their outdoor enclosure more pleasant, we moved a dead tree from the perimeter of the zoo and cemented it into a seven-foot hole so that the gorillas had somewhere to climb, which would give them much-needed exercise plus a vantage point from which they could see for miles across the zoo and the Leicestershire countryside.

When moving day came we had it all planned. Because Joe was so fond of going for a drive, despite the fact that he now weighed 150 lb, I led him out to the car and drove him the few yards to his new home, pulling up with his passenger door directly opposite to the door of the Gorilla House.

Playing Joe at his old game, I then instructed one of the keepers to bring Katy the cow up from her paddock. 'When you get here, shove her head through the window,' I shouted, winding down my window and hanging on to Joe's lead.

As Katy's head appeared through the window, Nat opened Joe's door and he shot out of the car, dragging me straight into the Gorilla House. Nat quickly shut the door behind us and, before Joe could get his bearings, I whipped off his collar and lead and skedaddled, leaving him staring after me. I then repeated the journey with Bongo – a trip made easier by virtue of the fact that, seeing her friend already installed in the new House, she allowed herself to be led into her section and settled down quite happily. Their chimp companions, Soco and Tina, joined them and the four resumed their usual life together, with the added benefits of larger living quarters and a more interesting outdoor play zone.

In the summer they sunbathed on the grass in the sunshine, never ceasing to be highly entertained by the antics of the visitors. Joe's great delight was to wait quietly in a corner of his room until there was a crowd peering through the glass partition and suddenly rush headlong at it, hitting it with all the force of his body and scattering his audience, who were terrified that he would come through the glass. This gave him endless amusement.

His other main pleasure was his sunken bath and he would splash around happily in it for hours, while Bongo, unwashed and unrepentant, passed her time mindlessly watching endless television programmes.

As Joe's behaviour became rougher, Soco his chimp companion became more and more unhappy with his violent play and constant teasing. It was time, we decided, that the two chimps should return to the chimp quarters, especially as the two gorillas were maturing and we hoped would mate and breed our first baby gorilla.

This was not to be. Although Joe is a magnificent specimen

of a Silverback Gorilla and grew to weigh over 400 lb, he has never shown any interest in mating with Bongo or any other female gorilla. Once again our breeding plans were thwarted.

CHAPTER FIFTEEN

Our Ape Quartet

We were not downhearted for long. Determined to locate a group of breeding gorillas, we put out feelers and eventually found a group at a dealer's in Holland. It was 1980 and by now, thankfully, there were stringent import controls in place to prevent zoos taking gorillas or any other endangered species from the wild. These particular animals by virtue of already being captive did not fall into this category. After being granted import licences and having our plans for quarantine quarters at the zoo passed by the Ministry, we were given permission to import two young females and a male, all of whom were very tame. The breeding pair were for Twycross and the third young gorilla was destined to go to Bristol Zoo after serving his quarantine time with us.

After a few months we were delighted to discover that our three new gorillas were *all* females – which upset the supplier greatly because females are of far greater value than males.

While they were still in quarantine we set about locating a young male gorilla to complete our breeding trio and found just what we were looking for at Gerald Durrell's Jersey Zoo, which had a surplus of male gorillas. Even so, things were not straightforward because their two young males, Asumbo and Mamfe, were inseparable and the zoo insisted that, if we wanted one, we had to take the other, too.

We had no alternative but to agree.

Mamfe, a fine Silverback Lowland Gorilla, was born at

Jersey Zoo in 1973. He is the son of Jambo, the famous gorilla who protected a young boy who fell into the enclosure from the other gorillas until he could be rescued. The two males settled in with our two females and, once out of quarantine, they took up residence in the main Gorilla House which was divided into two large day rooms with sleeping quarters. The de-luxe accommodation with the colour television and sunken bath was still occupied by Joe and Bongo, while Mamfe, Biddy and Eva took up residence in the other side.

Once they were acclimatised to each other, Bongo was allowed leave Joe and join the others, where she took on the role of surrogate mother, bringing a stabilising influence to the group with her gentle nature and love of babies. Joe, because of his incredible strength and unpredictability, was only allowed to watch them through the bars, but he seemed to be highly amused by their games and antics!

To our great delight, Mamfe fathered our very first gorilla baby – a bonny female born in 1985 called Asante. We were thrilled when we realised that Mamfe had mated with Eva. In order to confirm that she was pregnant we washed the tiled floor until it was spotless and waited for our prospective mother to urinate on to it, when we could collect a urine sample in a syringe and carry out a pregnancy test with the same kind of kit which is sold over the counter in pharmacies.

We were overjoyed when the test showed up positive. We were now expecting our first gorilla baby, and as with all our previous first births, we monitored Eva's progress closely, especially in the latter stages of her pregnancy when we kept a constant watch. Our diligence paid off and we were there when she went into labour and witnessed a little grey bundle of fur make its entrance into the world.

Unfortunately, Eva did not appear to be endowed with any maternal instinct and she left the newly born on the shelf. When it began crying she returned to it and we breathed a sigh of relief. Perhaps Nature was taking over, after all. We were dreadfully wrong and watched with growing horror as Eva picked it up in her foot and proceeded to walk round on it, wearing the newly-born baby like a shoe. By now the infant was in great distress and we had no alternative but to tranquillise Eva and remove the baby.

When we managed to take her away, the tiny animal was very cold and we were alarmed to see that she was passing blood; we feared that she had suffered internal injuries. We took her into the house and placed her on a heated pad to keep her warm. At first it was touch and go, and for the first four nights Nat took Asante to bed with her to give her the constant attention she needed. Eventually, to our relief, our battered baby made good progress and once more we ended up with yet another baby gorilla in the house.

At the time, we were becoming rather overcrowded in the orphan area. Not only did we have Asante, but we also had baby orang Leehee, Becky the baby chimp and, to complete the quartet, a baby Pileated Gibbon called Jason. Never before had we had babies of each species being brought up alongside each other at the same time. It was fascinating to see them all growing up together, and as youngsters they did not seem to realise that they were in any way different from each other – even though the orang had long, wispy red hair, the chimp had black hair and the gorilla, grey hair. They did have two things in common, however; their mothers had rejected them and they were all apes.

Like all orang babies, Leehee's wisps of hair stood on end and the others thought it was great fun to pull it. Each of them wore nappies including the gibbon, which had to have special small ones packed with wads of cotton wool. We realised what it must be like to have quads when it came to feeding time and they had to have a bottle each, and at night they each had a hug rug as a comforter.

As soon as they had progressed from the baby stage to

boisterous youngsters they would run up and down the stairs peering through the banisters. The only room they were not allowed in was the lounge. This time we wanted to keep our precious television set intact.

The differences between the four species became more apparent as they grew older.

As Asante grew in size, she behaved more like a gorilla, losing interest in toys and wanting to break things and rush around the house. Becky the chimp was fascinated by clothes and any new toys, and would delight in being shown how to use a hammer or to fit plastic shapes into a box as a human child would do. Leehee the orang would watch intently but was more interested in slowly examining the toys than doing anything with them. Out of all of them, Jason the gibbon was the most affectionate and gentle and it was he who had to be separated from the group first. By now they were a year old and Asante was getting much too rough to play with the others.

Fortunately, we had another gibbon the same age as our house-reared one and we gradually introduced the two by putting them in adjoining cages until they accepted each other. Once they had established a friendship they were allowed to play on the climbing frames in the gibbon enclosure for part of the day until the transition could become permanent.

The apes remained in the house for another few months until they were integrated with their own groups. I think that year, when all four babies lived with us, was the most hectic period we had ever experienced. There was not a minute's peace. After they moved out we breathed a sigh of relief, but the place seemed strangely quiet and empty.

After having fathered Asante, Mamfe went on to sire a male gorilla, Mambie, in 1991 and another daughter, Ozala, in 1994. These young gorillas form part of the 80 per cent of all gorillas who live in British zoos that are captive bred.

Mambie was the first gorilla baby that our gorilla keeper, Teresa, had ever been fortunate enough to see being born.

Ten years later he was to break her heart. By then, Asante, Mambie and another youngster named Tiger, later shortened to Ti, were living in relative harmony until for no apparent reason the two males began to fight and it was the more passive Ti who came off worst.

Teresa has always had an amazing rapport with the gorillas and, although there is a definite element of danger in going in with them, she chose that option. She was able to go in and play with gorillas twice her size and sometimes just in fun they would get too rough. She never blamed them and always said that it must be awfully difficult for them to curb their natural instincts. If they accidentally played too boisterously and she remonstrated with them, they would always stop.

When the really hard play-fighting between Ti and Mambie began in earnest, it was just as well that Teresa could go in with them and separate them by telling them off. By this time Ti was ten years old and had always been easygoing, due to the fact that he had been hand-reared, but Teresa was worried about his physical condition.

His appetite was insatiable, combined with which he had a pot belly which was hard to the touch. She felt that this was becoming a serious problem and that the other male gorilla was taking advantage and provoking fights. In the past their little altercations had been quite placid; now they were getting more serious as Mambie tried to establish himself as top gorilla.

I contacted Roger Coley about Ti's problem and he took the gorilla's plight quite seriously when he made his weekly visit to the zoo. By now, Ti's stomach was still hard and distended, but despite his enormous appetite he was losing weight and his backbone was beginning to protrude.

Roger's first instinct was that Ti was suffering from some kind of liver problem and should be anaesthetised to undergo extensive tests to locate the cause of the trouble. Ultrasound was used to scan the liver to see if there was any sign of a tumour or any other abnormality, but nothing showed up. Nor did blood tests reveal the cause of Ti's distress.

Meanwhile, at Roger's suggestion, the two male gorillas were separated and it was decided that Mambie should be found another home. If it came to a choice between the two, Mambie had to be the one to go because he was related to our female, Asante, and it was preferable that Ti should sire any offspring so that they were not inbred.

Finding a suitable home for Mambie was left to our Zoo Manager, John Ray. His task was not an easy one as male gorillas by now were extremely common, but eventually Paignton Zoo agreed that Mambie should join their bachelor group of gorillas.

It was not ideal and not what I or Teresa had hoped for. The only consolation was that he was going to a super home. Everyone would have preferred him to go somewhere where he would have been able to raise his own family, but perhaps that may happen in the future.

The day Mambie left for Paignton was very sad as we rarely part with any of our primates, and when he was tranquillised, the night before he left for his new home, to be moved into his travelling crate, we were all upset; particularly the person closest to him, Teresa.

We always encourage our keepers to become attached to their animals and treat them as their own, and Teresa is one of the keepers who has bonded extremely well with her charges. They may not be your children, but they *are* your friends, and so she had mixed feelings when Mambie was driven away from Twycross. She went with him to help him settle into his new home but even so it was a terrible wrench for her.

The only consolation was that from the moment Ti and Mambie were separated, Ti's tummy stopped being so distended, and even though his appetite had not abated he was far more happy and contented. The vet could only conclude that Ti had been suffering from stress caused by the friction between himself and Mambie.

While our other gorillas continued to breed, our

magnificent Silverback Joe consistently refused to take any interest in the females to whom he was introduced. Sadly, from his own choice Joe has remained a loner, choosing to live a monastic life in solitary splendour alongside other gorillas that he can see but cannot touch. Perhaps after observing the others' relationships he decided a bachelor life was simpler – women would only cause problems.

Our increasing population of gorillas presented us with a familiar problem. They had long since outgrown the wonderful Gorilla House we had been so proud to erect twenty years previously and it was high time for a new one. Given that the funds were available – amazingly! – it seemed simply a matter of deciding on the design and carrying out the work. A wildly optimistic assumption. As with all our previous building schemes, nothing could be further from the truth.

This time, red tape got in the way and confused matters. How do you set about planning a purpose-built Gorilla House? First you find a builder, put in your planning application and wait for the problems. The average time for plans to be passed is three months. The cost of building? Always allow at least one third above the original estimate and don't expect anything to be simple, cut and dried. The following is an example of the kind of red tape we had to deal with.

The colour of the brick and roof tiles had to be taken to the council for approval. We had deliberately chosen brick that matched the other buildings nearby. The Council said they would prefer us to use a darker brick. We had two choices, to accept gracefully or to go to appeal.

Opting for the first meant we wouldn't get what we wanted. Opting for the second – appeal – meant the start of the building could be delayed by another three months.

'How about the roofing tile which matches the Elephant House?'

'No, that would not be suitable because the Planning Officer prefers the other one.'

Defeated and deflated, we accepted their choice and our builders got down to digging out the foundations. No problems here, we thought naively. After all, there are no trees in the vicinity, therefore no tree roots.

We informed the Building Inspector that the foundations were dug out, only to be told that because of the height of the building they must go down at least two feet deeper. Keeping our thoughts to ourselves, we complied with his request.

Eventually, after all the teething troubles, the Gorilla House was well underway. The roof was put on and everyone breathed a sigh of relief. Too soon. New problems had arisen. The slits for the lights were restricted to being four feet long, but to give adequate lighting, a six-feet length was required.

'You cannot do that – it will weaken the structure of the building,' we were told. Again we chose discretion and accepted the decision of the experts, only to be proved right: the lighting was *not* adequate.

The design of the day places included two sunken baths which initially we viewed with pride – until we noticed that although the water had been laid on, there was no method of emptying them. There was no plug-hole!

'Experts' were called in to do the underfloor heating and once again there were setbacks. The electric cable was duly installed and the floor tiles laid, but when the heating was tested we discovered that it was totally inadequate. This caused a big upheaval as the whole system had to be altered and improved to reach the required temperature.

When all of these difficulties had been eliminated and the House was finally finished, we turned to the outside enclosure (for which we didn't need planning permission) and we heaved a sigh of relief. *Too soon*. Because of the height of the wall, we had to have a stresses and strains assessment, only to be told that it would need to be reinforced with steel girders. By this time we were pretty stressed out ourselves and didn't realise that a wall could suffer from the same affliction.

Any enclosure must have 'environmental enrichment' so we put advertisements in local newspapers for big trees. There were plenty of oak trees within a hundred-mile radius, but the cost of transport was either too prohibitive, or the tree was too large, too small or too rotten to be any use. Eventually, after weeks of advertising and elimination, suitable trees were found and transported. But big trees need a big hole, a digger to dig it, tons of concrete to stabilise them and a crane to lift them into position.

Next we needed play equipment and a firm was approached that makes equipment from logs for children's playgrounds. A design was agreed and the strength of the gorillas was impressed upon the manufacturer. Everything must be bolted firmly together, we stipulated, or it would disintegrate.

Platform, bars and a small cabin arrived and were put in position. They looked fine, except they were held together with four-inch nails, it transpired, and alterations had to be carried out pronto while our frustrated keepers looked on.

After months of setbacks and misery we were finally able to stand back and look at our new Gorilla House. Everything was in place, the play area was fully equipped, even the grass had grown, and now all we had to do was move our eight gorillas from their old House on the other side of the zoo to their new habitat.

Two vets and a veterinary nurse were in attendance when the operation began. One vet took up his post in the old Gorilla House with tranquillisers at the ready to sedate each gorilla, while the other vet and the veterinary nurse were despatched to the brand new House with other medical equipment.

The gorillas were tranquillised one by one with a blow dart, placed on a stretcher and carried out to a waiting van by two keepers who accompanied them in the back while the driver drove the short distance across the zoo to their new abode. Awaiting their arrival were the other vet and nurse, who proceeded to examine each of them carefully, looking at their teeth and taking blood samples while they were still unconscious before giving them an injection to bring them round.

The whole procedure took just two hours, with Joe still in his own separate sleeping quarters, day enclosure and outside play area while Mamfe was head of the main group which consisted of Bongo, Biddy, Eva and Ozala, who was born into the group.

The new House and enclosures met with their approval, which was very gratifying, and we are now hoping that in the twenty-first century even more gorilla babies will be conceived.

CHAPTER SIXTEEN

Making Love, Not War

San Diego Zoo in California and its adjoining Wildlife
Park are world famous, a Mecca for animal lovers,
zoologists and zoo keepers who flock to see its collection
of mammals, birds and reptiles which is the largest in
North America. The zoo is home, in fact, to a staggering
1,607 mammals – many of which are endangered, but
thanks to the experts there conducting some of the world's
most successful breeding programmes, those rare species
continue to flourish.

Like many other people involved with zoos, every time
Nat and I pack our bags to go on holiday we head for
another zoo, to meet old friends, to keep up with the latest
trends, and more importantly, to see their animals.

The curators at San Diego Park are old friends, their
work in breeding programmes over the years exceptional,
with many of the births at the zoo first-time successes. Of
course, the real attraction of the zoo for Nat and myself are
the thirty-three species of primates, which include a
breeding group of gorillas and the largest successfully
breeding group of Pygmy Chimps in North America.

The thing we were most looking forward to on this
particular trip in 1990 was to come face to face for the first
time with real live Bonobos – an encounter which proved
every bit as thrilling as when we saw our first chimp. Most
people have still never heard of these apes, who are
closely related to chimps yet in many ways are far more
like humans than any other primate.

It is less than a hundred years ago that Bonobos were

discovered living in the heart of the hot, wet swamps of Zaire, the only area in the wild where they exist.

Smaller and more slender than chimps, they are extremely rare and endangered, their numbers dwindling, and American scientists who are studying them believe there may only be 10,000 still living in the wild. There are just 200 in breeding programmes in zoos worldwide.

Some scientists have hailed them as 'the missing link', our closest cousins – and certainly, watching them in their family group in San Diego Zoo, the resemblance to humans was uncanny. They look more like us than the other apes. Their heads are smaller than chimps' heads, their necks slimmer, their facial features more delicate; they lack the big eye-teeth of chimpanzees and have red lips like humans. The hair on their bodies is sleeker and finer than that of a chimp, and although they do lope around on all fours, when they stop and stand up their posture is as upright as ours.

Seeing them standing there staring at us was most disconcerting; they were *so much* like humans! No wonder every zoo would like to have its own breeding group and we were no exception, which is why we were excited months later when I received an invitation to go to Antwerp to attend a meeting of the qualified scientific committee that decides where endangered species should be placed on loan. In this case they were interviewing prospective zoo directors to decide their suitability to have a group of Bonobos on breeding loan.

Plans to rehouse some of our older chimps were immediately put on hold. The former Elephant House for which they had been destined had just been especially converted, with two large indoor areas, three bedplaces at each end, and an outside enclosure with a dry-moated grass island, a waterfall and a small pool with trees and ropes for climbing. This resembled as closely as possible an environment which would be ideal for Bonobos.

Armed with photographs and detailed plans, I arrived at the meeting in Antwerp. Even so I was unprepared for the grilling which lay ahead. I faced a dozen eminent council members who wanted to know every detail about our zoo and our plans for the Bonobos. They were charming and polite but left no stone unturned in ensuring we were suitable to take in the rare primates.

I was none the wiser when I left two days later to return to Twycross. Any hope that they would make a quick decision was dashed when they informed us that they would make their deliberations and be in touch. Almost a year had passed when I was summoned to appear once more before the same council in Antwerp. Again everything was talked over but I felt they were no nearer making up their minds until I leaned across the table and said, 'Excuse me, but do you *want* me to have the Bonobos? Because if not, then I have some chimps waiting to move into their accommodation.'

Prompted by my question, it took them just twenty minutes to decide that they would let us have a breeding group of four, which meant that Twycross would be the first British zoo to be given such an honour.

The group we would have on loan consisted of a twelve-year-old male called Kakowet II who had been born at San Diego Zoo, a fifteen-year-old female called Diatou, born at Stuttgart Zoo, and her three-year-old daughter Kichele, also born at Stuttgart Zoo, and a two-year-old male, Jasongo, who had been born at Wüppertal Zoo. I was also asked if I could take in Kuni, a seven-year-old female, for a year until she could travel to take up residence in the new Bonobo House which was in the process of being built in San Diego.

The Bonobos would be accompanied on their journey by two of their keepers, who would stay at Twycross for a week to see them settled in and give valuable advice on their welfare to our keepers.

Everyone at the zoo was thrilled at the thought of having the Bonobos and our excitement grew on the day of their arrival when we saw a lorry with five crates and two keepers coming up the drive.

We lost no time in unloading them as they were obviously stressed and tired by their journey, particularly the two younger ones, but their placid temperament helped as their keepers reassured them and helped to settle them down. As we watched them gradually relax and snuggle into their beds, it suddenly dawned on us that we had overlooked a major problem. The keepers spoke to them in German; Twycross keepers spoke only English. However would we get over the language barrier?

During the following week our keepers not only had to introduce themselves and become accepted by the Bonobos, they also had to learn the German phrases which meant so much to them.

It was a great upheaval for the Bonobo group, for not only did they have to get to know their new surroundings and the keepers, but with the exception of Diatou and her daughter Kichele, they had come from different backgrounds and had to get to know each other. That they achieved harmony so quickly was a tribute to their passive nature – and to a television set.

Television sets are installed in all of the Ape Houses to provide entertainment and stimulation, and the moment the Bonobos spotted theirs in the corner they were mesmerised. For a whole week they sat in front of the set, riveted; even when food was provided, they just reached out for a piece of fruit or vegetable, their eyes never leaving the screen. At the end of the week they had formed a bond and sorted themselves into a family group, with Kakowet taking over as a father figure caring for the two youngsters while the two older females in true Bonobo fashion had palled up together.

Unlike chimps and other apes, Bonobo society is governed by the females, who form a strong sisterhood, punishing any male who dares to attack a female by jumping to her rescue and setting on him. They also control the food, having first choice while the males stay at a safe distance until they are allowed their share.

On the other hand, Bonobo males rarely form any

attachments with their own sex, not even banding together to defend themselves. Their differences are settled by sex. The Bonobo philosophy of 'Make love, not war' diffuses any confrontational situations and relieves stresses and tensions by the sex act.

Our Bonobos were no exception, and if any problem reared up, they would immediately have sex, even the little ones. Their sexual activities differ from those of any other monkey or ape, for they have as many sexual variations as the Kamasutra. Only Man can equal their sexual ingenuity.

This kind of society is a complete contrast to that of chimpanzees, where males totally dominate their females and enjoy nothing better than a good fight, when they will put on an awe-inspiring display, rushing around screaming and banging and thumping anything which gets in their way.

In the wild they fight viciously and will join together to kill any strange chimp, whereas film of Bonobos in the wild have shown that when they meet up with another group there is much nervous shrieking but no physical confrontation. Again it is the female hierarchy who make the first approaches and introduce themselves by initiating sexual advances to each other.

Bonobo expert Dr France de Wall, who wrote *Bonobo – The Forgotten Chimp*, encapsulates the difference between the two species in this observation: 'Common chimps resolve sexual issues with power. Bonobos resolve power issues with sex.'

I would agree with that description of sex playing a major role in Bonobo philosophy, but my own way of summing up the difference in their intelligence is to say that while chimps would go to an ordinary comprehensive, Bonobos would go to a university.

Our Bonobos were a delightfully peace-loving group and although we could not have the same confidence and freedom to go in with them as we did with the individual chimps we had brought up from babies, they did respond to our keepers and ourselves. They would talk in their high-pitched, twittering, bird-like voices and would take food from our hands and offer us presents.

Bonobos are uncannily like us in their ability to size up situations; they can sometimes be devious enough to take advantage of it, but they are also tender and loving, like humans. Because of their intelligence, a great deal of thought had gone into the design of the Bonobo House at Twycross. It had a sunken bath, swings, rope ladders and hammocks and also an imitation termite hill made from a rock. In the centre was a large pot of yoghurt and the Bonobos lost no time in working out that if they pushed sticks through the holes drilled in the rock's exterior they could reach the yoghurt, and they spent many happy hours busily feeding themselves this treat.

Another device to occupy them was to insert baby food into the cracks of their wooden uprights around the enclosure, which kept them busy and interested, picking out the food with slender sticks. These tricks made them hunt for food as they would have done in their natural habitat, which was very desirable. I have to admit here that it did not take the Bonobos as long to find the food and tease it out as it did for our keepers to put it there!

Betty and Marcus, the two keepers who first looked after the Bonobos, spent most of their time trying to devise activities to keep these clever creatures stimulated. One of their favourite foods is sugar cane, and in the wild Bonobos will raid sugar-cane plantations and decimate the crops. They are treated as scavengers by farmers, who combat these raiding parties by shooting them like vermin.

Sugar cane at the zoo is presented to them in a far different guise. Betty thought up the idea of placing the sugar cane in bowls and floating them on the pool in their enclosure. The Bonobos were happy to wade into the water to retrieve their treat, unlike chimps, who would not enter the water no matter what the inducement.

Like everyone who comes into contact with the Bonobos, Betty loved them and became totally wrapped up in the Bonobo way of life.

'It's so lovely to watch their family groups, they have such a beautiful society. I envy them,' she has often told me. 'The Bonobos are charming, they never grow up and never take life seriously. It's an ideal society where females are dominant. What more could you want?'

Certainly, observing Bonobo behaviour has given us plenty of pleasant surprises. I well remember the day that a starling had somehow managed to get into the indoor day quarters of the animals.

If this had been chimp quarters he would have received a very different reception and would have been taking his life into his hands. On one dreadful occasion a bird had invaded the chimps' space and was hunted and killed, and the chimp responsible wore its feathers triumphantly on his head like a Red Indian head-dress for a day before we could retrieve them.

By contrast, when one of the Bonobos, Diatou, spotted the visiting starling, she went over and caught it, then folding its wings gently back as an experienced bird fancier would do, she carefully carried it out and, holding it in her hands, released it and watched it fly away.

Another instance of caring interaction was when a nine-year-old female Bonobo called Banya arrived on loan from Cologne Zoo. She was very aloof and would not come down from her shelf for three days. She even refused to come down for food and just stayed on her shelf looking miserable. Suddenly one of the young Bonobos detached himself from the rest of the group, took some food and water over to her and placed it on a nearby shelf, just as a caring person might do to help a stranger.

My favourite of the group was Kuni, and even though I knew that she was only with us for a year, I grew extremely attached to her and dreaded the thought of her leaving. I felt so desperately sorry for her when she left. If only we could have explained to her why she was being taken from her new family group and being packed into a crate to face a long flight to San Diego. I would have been even more upset if I had realised that this sociable, intelligent animal would now have to spend six months in quarantine, in solitary confinement.

But within weeks my attention was diverted back to our Bonobo family when we discovered that Diatou was pregnant. We were unable to pinpoint the exact date that she conceived due to the fact that she and Kakowet had regular sex anyway. Bonobos only breed every four years if they have a baby, and now that Kichele was four years old we had expected Diatou to start ovulating again. We could only estimate that the birth would take place between eight and nine months. In fact it was eight and a half months later, during the night of 2 January 1994, that Diatou gave birth to a male infant, who we named Ke Ke, the first birth of the species in the UK.

We had no idea how long Diatou had been in labour as he was born at night, and by the time the keeper found them, Mother and Baby were doing fine. Ke Ke was already suckling from his mother while the rest of the group crowded round, watching the proceedings intently but making no attempt to touch the newborn.

For the next six weeks the Bonobos would continue to gather round solicitously, like a human family taking interest in a new member. During this time our keeper, Betty, kept a careful note of the baby's progress and saw the very first major interaction which took place when Diatou placed Ke Ke on the ground and allowed his father Kakowet and his half-sister Kichele to play with him. For a few minutes they all gently touched his fingers and tickled him.

Until he was three months old Ke Ke did little except hold on to his mother and suckle. By then he could hold small things in his hands and was taking an interest in the other members of the family, holding his hand out to touch them.

The next significant milestone was at four months when he learned to crawl, his limbs splayed out at an angle, and he began to spend more and more time off his mother's breast. All this progress had been closely watched by

Kichele, who one day dived at Ke Ke and snatched him up and ran off with him with Diatou in hot pursuit, retrieving him in seconds before giving Kichele a sharp slap. However, within a week, having ingratiated herself with her mother Diatou by grooming her, Kichele was allowed to take the infant and keep him with her for a few minutes. Even then Diatou, like any good mother, stayed very close and kept a close watch on her two offspring.

We were very proud of our first baby Bonobo's progress and watched his first attempt at standing on all fours with all the pride of any parent. By the time he was eight months old, Ke Ke was able to stand upright on his two feet with the aid of Kakowet and Kichele, who would hold his hands just as we would a human child.

But I had not forgotten Kuni. That year Nat and I decided to pay another visit to San Diego Zoo and my first objective was to visit the Bonobo enclosure to see our old friend.

San Diego Zoo and Wildlife Park is in two sections and when we arrived at the Bonobo section of the zoo we were told that Kuni had been transferred to the group of Bonobos at the Wildlife Park. Trying to hide our disappointment, we decided to visit her the following day and have a look around the zoo area. As we stood amongst the crowds in front of the Bonobo enclosure debating our plans, we noticed that one female Bonobo kept staring at us before detaching herself from the group and coming over towards us. She paused for a moment to break off a twig from a branch before approaching and offering it to us.

'That Bonobo knows you,' an onlooker said. He was right. It was Kuni.

We had not recognised her, yet two years on and after all the thousands of people she had seen, this intelligent creature had known us amongst the crowds and brought us a gift. It was very touching.

Three years later at Twycross, Diatou gave birth to a

female baby, Yasa, and we were overjoyed that we had once more successfully bred another endangered Bonobo. For endangered they are. Despite all the care and conservation amongst world zoos to preserve the species, these intelligent creatures are being decimated by the destruction of their natural habitat as more and more areas of forest are cut down for logging. Viruses brought in by Man are also taking their toll on animals that have not built up any resistance to these foreign bugs.

Even more horrific is the fact that in spite of their rarity they, alongside chimps, monkeys and elephants, are still being killed for bushmeat, not to feed starving natives but to be exported as a delicacy to restaurants in cities in Africa and to France and Italy.

A friend of ours visited a restaurant in South America and ordered a very nice stew. When she praised the chef's cooking she was taken back to the kitchen where she was horrified to find that the main ingredient of her meal had been a rare Spider Monkey. The bodies of others were hanging up waiting to go into the pot.

Stories of these horrors made us realise just how important it is to ensure the survival of the species by breeding them in captivity, which is why we were delighted when in 1998 Kichele, Diatou's daughter, became pregnant and we looked forward to a third-generation Bonobo being born.

This time the keepers kept a twenty-four-hour watch on the expectant mum and saw her go into labour in late afternoon. By evening the Bonobos began making their individual nests from wood wool and, though perfectly aware of what was happening, just carried on with their normal routine until just before the baby was born, when they gathered around and watched the delivery without interfering.

To our dismay, when the baby was born it was perfectly obvious that it was dead. The umbilical cord was wrapped tightly around its neck. Kichele looked at his tiny body and went away, leaving it lying on the floor while the rest of the group gathered round the body and gently touched it until Kichele returned and picked it up and carried into the night quarters.

For the next eighteen hours the baby was tenderly cared for by the whole group. The two youngest Bonobos, Ke Ke and Yasa, tried to get its lifeless body to react by touching it carefully, and it was heartbreaking to see Kichele try to suckle it. The grief of the whole group was obvious. They were like a human family mourning the loss of a child.

The following day they decided they could not help it in any way and allowed the keeper to remove the body without any fuss.

Everyone at the zoo had been looking forward to the birth, and the disappointment and sadness at losing the baby was felt by all.

CHAPTER SEVENTEEN

My Friends the Monkeys

As I write these words, it is a beautiful spring morning and I can hear the gibbons greeting the sunrise. The *boom-boom* of the Siamangs as their throats swell up like a ball is followed by the different notes of the other gibbons – the Lar, Pileated, Agile and Concolor – as one sets the others off until there is a resonating chorus across the zoo.

Our collection of gibbons is one of the most popular of exhibits at Twycross and I like to walk through the House to catch a glimpse of the baby gibbons who are usually to be seen clinging to their mothers. Inside the Gibbon House is a very special Kloss Gibbon called Bilou, who came to us from Basle Zoo. They had once had a whole group of Kloss Gibbons there, but over the years they had all died out until only Bilou remained, destined to live out his life on his own. However, Bilou had a fairy godmother in the shape of Kathleen Tobler, who lived with her husband Luc in Switzerland.

Kathleen worked in the administration department of Basle Zoo and one of her main interests was the collections of monkeys there – in particular the rare Kloss Gibbons. This species is black in colour and is smaller than the other types of gibbon.

One day in 1979, we received a letter from Kathleen telling us of Bilou's solitary plight and asking if we would be prepared to give him a home and try to find him a mate. Of course, we agreed. Sorting out the details, applying for the permission and documentation to move Bilou, was all dealt with by Luc and Kathleen, who not only took that burden off our shoulders but also hired a private plane to fly Bilou to Birmingham Airport.

Kathleen herself spent days introducing Bilou to the special travelling crate she had made for the journey. Bilou was used to receiving a lot of care and attention both from zoo keepers and Kathleen, and so he was very bewildered when the day came for him to leave the Gibbon House which he had known all his life, to be put in the crate and then on to the plane which would take him to England.

We met the Toblers and Bilou at Birmingham Airport with our quarantine van and took him back to the zoo where he was to spend six months in quarantine on his own, which was no hardship to Bilou as he had grown accustomed to leading a solitary existence after the last members of his family died.

Kathleen, devoted as ever, stayed with him for the first week to help him settle in and also visited during the rest of his quarantine. After six months the Ministry vet examined him and pronounced that he was a healthy little fellow and safe to leave quarantine. That day we took him to the Gibbon House and installed him in a cage alongside a female Siamang Gibbon, hoping that when they got to know each other, they might become friends and companions.

Things never go according to plan, do they? Bilou was quite emphatic that he did not like Siamangs. She might be the same colour that he was, but she was *not* the same kind!

Over the years we have desperately tried to find a mate for Bilou and when we eventually located one in Australia, we were naturally very pleased. Our joy was short-lived though, since before they could obtain the necessary papers to export her to England, she died. Poor Bilou, still all alone.

Perhaps the gentleman preferred blondes, we wondered, and chose a nice, fawn-coloured female for him, but after a brief introduction he turned her down. He was *not* hybridising with another species, he seemed to be saying. He would tolerate them as neighbours – but a personal relationship was out of the question.

Bilou is now getting to be an old man but he still enjoys bachelor life. Kathleen visits him twice a year and he greets her like an old friend. The bond they forged is still there. He has never forgotten his early years when she looked after him and gave him extra special care.

Another of our monkey personalities is Randyman, a Red-faced Black Spider Monkey. We believe he is the oldest recorded member of his species ever known. He is at least forty-four years old, and we only have records on him which go back to 1958. Before that he was a pet on board a sailing ship and when he came to us at Hints he had a leather belt around his waist that was so tight it had become embedded in the flesh and had to be removed by the vet.

Randyman has been at Twycross ever since we opened, and although he has had several female companions he has never bred. Even at his advanced age he is still very agile and loves to swing from the branches and ropes in his enclosure. As he has grown older a few of his teeth have fallen out and his food has to be cut into tiny pieces by his keepers.

Randyman is a real character with an amazing memory and calls out to people he has not seen for years. This handsome monkey has the most amazingly clear blue eyes, while all the other Red-faced Black Spider Monkeys have brown eyes.

Across the way are the Javan Langurs who live in the nearby Langur House. They are very attractive with their vivid red hair, and very lively. There is also a black phase of the breed. They are a complete contrast to the spectacled langurs with their soft grey hair and white ringed eyes, which makes them look so appealing.

All of the langurs are very active, always on the go, spending a lot of time outside in their enclosures swinging from the tree branches which are designed to simulate their natural habitat. They are also devoted parents and spend hours feeding, grooming and caring for their babies.

Langurs are leaf-eating monkeys with an unusual digestive system. In captivity they are fed mainly on leaves and vegetables with an occasional egg or insect thrown in.

As I walk across the path I can see that the Spider Monkeys have been let out and are using their incredibly long arms to swing effortlessly around the trees in their enclosure. They, like the Woolly Monkeys, have a small black pad on the underside of their tail with which they can hold on to branches. This acts as another hand which enables them to hang upside down while they use their hands to pick up tasty morsels of nuts and yoghurt.

When a weird noise can be heard echoing across the zoo, it is picked up by another group over the way. It comes from the Red Howler Monkeys from South America, so named because of their vocalisation.

These are very special animals and we are very lucky to have them. On one of our trips to San Diego Zoo we were looking at some of their amazing exhibits when one of the directors sidled up and whispered in my ear, 'Would you like some Howler Monkeys?' and smiled at the look of joy on my face.

When they arrived at Twycross I was even more pleased. I had thought our director friend was offering us Black Howler Monkeys, which would have been more than acceptable. When I saw that he had meant the rarer Red Howlers I was deeply thrilled. Even more so, of course, when they successfully mated and bred.

Unfortunately, owing to there being so few in captivity, many Howler Monkeys are inbred or closely related to each other, which is not the ideal situation, as in the long term it can weaken their resistance to infection and cause abnormalities. If you see them you will always remember their striking coloration, and if you are lucky enough to hear them howl you will never forget it!

Today, we also have groups of Black Howler Monkeys

which have the same voice and the same pads on their tails, but they are not quite so striking. The males are black and the females are fawn in coloration.

In the Monkey House there is a very special old female monkey, a Red Uakari called Blossom, who is much more slender in build than the other monkeys: she has red hair and a bright red face which goes very pale if she is not well. Her mate died a few years ago and we had to pair her off with a very old Capuchin Monkey who died last year. I am hoping to find her a suitable companion as I think it is unfair to keep solitary animals. Like humans, they need company and stimulation.

Visitors can also see a group of spectacular black and white Colobus Monkeys. When the babies are born they are completely white, but change dramatically as they get older until they achieve the same black bodies, white capes and tail tips as their parents. I have always been fascinated to watch the white babies being passed from female to female; they act as aunts to the youngsters, teaching them nursery skills and how to socialise.

Opposite the Monkey House is *The World of Small Monkeys*. Here you will find Golden Lion Tamarins which are very endangered, but thanks to the breeding programmes in worldwide zoos, some have now been released back into the wild.

In the 1940s when there were no restrictions on imports, backstreet dealers had a profusion of species which are now on the highly endangered list and almost extinct, and I remember once seeing eighteen Golden Lion Tamarins in a cage in the grubby shop of a London dealer. At the time I had no idea how rare they would become; what I did recognise was that, kept in those conditions, the little monkeys stood little chance of survival. Today they would represent a large proportion of the world population of this species. How I wish that we had had enough money to buy them.

All groups of Golden Tamarins in zoos are the property of the Brazilian government; the animals are genetically

matched for breeding and moved around to where they
are required. Theirs is one of the success stories of zoos
rehabilitating them into the wild. Before the captive-bred
Golden Tamarins can be released, they have to go through
a period of rehabilitation where they learn to hang on to
moving branches and forage for food.

In the same House are Emperor Tamarins, Red-Bellied
Tamarins and Pygmy Marmosets – one of the smallest
monkeys – Silvery Marmosets and Goeldi Monkeys. They
may all look different, but they have one crucial thing in
common – a distinctive smell – and the fact that they are
the smallest of the monkey family.

As I do the rounds of the monkeys, the words of a poem
called *The Monkeys' Viewpoint* often spring to mind:

Three monkeys sat in a coconut tree
Discussing things that are said to be.
Said one to the others, 'Now listen, you two,
There's a certain rumour that cannot be true!
That man descended from our noble race.
The very idea is a dire disgrace!
No monkey ever deserted his wife
Starved his baby and ruined her life.
And another thing you'll never see
A monk' build a fence round a coconut tree
And let the coconuts go to waste
Forbidding all other monks' to taste.
Why, if I put a fence around this tree
Starvation would force you to steal from me.
Here's another thing a monk' won't do:
Go out at night and get in a stew
Or use a gun or club or knife
To take some other monkey's life.
Yes, man descended, the ornery cuss.
But brothers, he didn't descend from us!'

CHAPTER EIGHTEEN

Great Escapes

After my visit to the monkeys, I walk back past the paddocks, one of which contains a group of Alpaca. These belong to the Giraffe family but, unlike them, come from South America where, like the Llama, they have a dual purpose. Their wool is used to make warm clothes and they are also used as pack animals. Their long necks enable the alpaca to see me coming in the distance and they watch my approach with interest, hoping to be treated to a handful of zoo nuts. Their calves are already tucking into their morning hay.

Further along, the Capybaras, one of the largest rodents, have been up since daylight foraging around their paddock, followed by their five babies who run beside their parents as they would in the wild.

A pair of Brazilian Tapirs take a morning stroll around the succulent grass of their enclosure. The male is getting old but managed to sire a youngster last year. Tapir babies are born with stripes, which act as camouflage, blending in with dappled shadows in the Brazilian forests.

The late risers are the Barbirusa, who are only just waking up, their internal clocks set for when the keeper will arrive with their breakfast. The name Barbirusa is an Indonesian word meaning 'Pig-deer', because the curved tusks of the male resemble deer's antlers. These attractive animals look like slender pigs but with a longer, almost trunk-like snout. In fact, they are an entirely different species and are related to hippos; their stomach has four chambers rather like a cow's.

Over the last thirty-seven years there have been few escapes at Twycross, but those few have been memorable. The Barbirusas, I am afraid to say, are among the guilty parties. It was a time when Jim, their keeper, was away on holiday that one of the Barbirusas decided to make a bid for freedom by dodging between the legs of the cover keeper and fleeing into the zoo.

An immediate alert was radioed to the staff and the Emergency Drill leapt into action; all gates were shut as staff closed in on the escapee. Seeing his path blocked by gates, the Barbirusa changed direction and loped back the way it had come. The keeper trailing after him breathed a sigh of relief, thinking the animal was heading back for his enclosure.

All seemed well until the Barbirusa passed the Tiger Enclosure where, eyeing this tasty morsel, the tigers pounced at the wire, frightening the animal, who took off across the car park and from there went cross-country, heading for the local village.

Throughout the day the search continued, to no avail. Over the next few days there were various sightings of our Barbirusa and staff, armed with nets, were dispatched to catch it – but every time they arrived at the location the animal had disappeared. It was early summer with food and vegetation in abundance, so the Barbirusa was able to lead a happy, leisurely life roaming the countryside, moving from one farm and one village to another until finally deciding to make its home in Gopsall Woods, where there was plenty of cover and good rooting ground.

When Jim returned from holiday he was very upset and was determined that no matter how long it took or how many miles he travelled, he would get his Barbirusa back.

He spent hours tramping around the fields loyally looking for the enterprising escapee. The Barbirusa is about as big as a medium-sized pig but grey in colour, which helped it to blend into any background. After two weeks of freedom it was also extremely fit and could outrun any pursuers. Once it was tracked down to its new abode in Gopsall Woods, this gave Jim the opportunity to lay a trap for it.

Scanning the undergrowth, the keeper could detect the areas which the Barbirusa visited on a regular basis and he began leaving food for it each day. When the food started to disappear Jim hoped and prayed that his plan would work – for the Barbirusa was now becoming accustomed to being fed.

Already Jim had designed a trap which consisted of a large, upturned wooden box propped up on a forked stick which had a long string attached. Each day the food was placed under the box while Jim played a waiting game, allowing the wary Barbirusa to become accustomed to this strange shelter-cum-feeding station. Jim's strategy and patience were eventually rewarded. Hiding in the undergrowth, he held his breath as the Barbirusa unsuspectingly walked past him straight into the box and began to eat. Knowing that he would only have one chance of trapping his quarry, Jim gave a mighty tug on the string, yanking the stick from under the wooden crate and trapping the Barbirusa inside.

A call for help and other keepers arrived to help carry the box back through the woods to the road and a waiting van.

When the Barbirusa arrived back at the zoo it wasn't tired, it wasn't hungry, it had just had a good holiday in the country and returned fit and well, much to the relief of us all.

Another escapee from the paddocks was a female Malayan Tapir. Tapirs are timid, nocturnal creatures related to horses and rhinos and are approximately three feet in height. Their bodies are stocky and, in the case of the Malayan Tapir, are black with a broad white band over their loins and rump; they also have small rounded ears and a short, movable trunk.

Despite weighing a massive 200 lb, our fugitive tapir was an incredibly fast mover. We first discovered she was missing when a keeper noticed that the wire on the front of the Tapir enclosure had been lifted. To this day we don't know whether this was done by the tapir herself or whether some irresponsible human had a hand in effecting her escape. Certainly tapirs, with their sensitive noses, do not have the capacity to dig their way out, but this one had not only managed to get out into the zoo but from there had made off across the busy main road into the farmer's field opposite.

A general alert went out to all keepers, who parked a van across the road, straddling it. Two keepers stopped the traffic one way while another three keepers directed traffic on the other side. Our vet, who was on the premises, the curator and two other keepers with nets and tranquilliser guns followed the tapir as she ran across the fields jumping over ditches – some of which her pursuers managed to fall into. Eventually, hot and dishevelled, they were able to turn the tapir back in the direction of the zoo.

On her return journey, the harassed tapir also fell headlong into one of the ditches. At this point the posse of keepers decided it might not be a good idea to tranquillise her as it would be difficult to carry an animal weighing around 16 stone on a stretcher across the rough terrain.

They waited for some minutes until the tapir finally heaved her bulk out of the ditch and slowly lumbered back through the hedge across the road towards the waterfowl pools in the zoo. By this time she was bewildered and frightened by her escapade. As she saw the vet and keepers closing in, she flung herself at the perimeter hedge which bordered the zoo, bulldozed her way through and plunged into the pool.

Tapirs love water, and as she paddled and floundered around we all gave a sigh of relief. Of course, we still had the problem of getting her into her enclosure, but at least she was back in the zoo.

The curator and vet nobly waded into the muddy water up to their chests and drove her towards a specially prepared gap in the fence. With gentle persuasion the tapir was returned to her own enclosure, where she was rewarded with a tasty meal. The keepers were left to repair and secure the fences while the sodden vet and curator, covered in extremely smelly mud, went off to change their clothes and revive themselves with cups of coffee. The excitement over, everyone went back to their normal duties while the tapir settled down for the rest of the day in a deep bed of straw to sleep off her exertions.

Despite all our stringent precautions at Twycross, with automatic doors, locks and alarms, there is always an element of human error, which can thwart the best-laid plans. I have been guilty of this myself when in one distracted moment an opportunist chimp called Josie took advantage.

Josie had a chequered background before she arrived at Twycross. As a baby she had been stolen from Dudley Zoo and after police searches in the locality had been discovered, still in her box, in the ladies' toilets in Wolverhampton. She was being hand-reared and was so young that she could not walk.

As we were already hand-rearing other chimps of that age, Dudley Zoo asked if we would take her in, and like her two companions, twelve-year-old Flynn and Becky, she was brought up in the house and now lives with them in the chimp quarters nearest to it.

All three are the most delightful chimps, especially Flynn, and although it is dangerous to go in with adult chimps, especially a fully-grown male with his females, I am still very relaxed about entering their indoor quarters although Nat is always warning me against it. She often says that one day people will go in and find just my shoelaces. In particular she has never trusted Josie and her instincts were proved right when one day we were at their House and I opened the door to the inside enclosure to let Josie into her bedplace, upon which she sailed out of the door and charged down into the zoo.

Nat and I lost no time in jumping into our cars to give

chase. We cautiously followed her progress as she loped casually from one exhibit to another as if she were any visitor out for a stroll. Her first stop was at the Flamingo Pool, where she watched intently the long-legged pink birds paddling in their lake. I felt that her interest was far from aesthetic; she was more likely eyeing them up as a prospective dinner, but they were quite safe as chimps will not go through water. Josie continued to roam round, followed now by other keepers as well as ourselves. After half an hour, aware now that she was being stalked, she headed for the grassed enclosure belonging to the orang utans. To our horror she jumped on to the top of the glass barrier and took a flying leap into the enclosure. We all breathed more easily when we realised that, by a lucky chance, none of the orangs were out, but were safely shut into their indoor quarters. Only the door to one empty indoor heated area was open and Josie made for that. She climbed up on to one of the top shelves eight feet above the ground and made herself at home there. The vet was on the premises and arrived with tranquillising equipment which is kept locked in the house. The reclining Josie was an easy target; the vet took aim and one bulls-eye later a startled Josie slumped down on the shelf.

It took two men and a ladder to get her down from her exalted perch and she was wheeled back to her own home in a wheelbarrow.

It was Bongo, our female gorilla who had been brought up in the house, who gave me my biggest fright. After years of wrecking most of our furniture and possessions, when she and Joe were moved into their custom-built gorilla quarters we settled down to a more peaceful existence and began replacing items they had destroyed. For once we revelled in shopping for ornaments and pictures to brighten up the lounge.

We even commissioned a portrait of Ozala, with Bongo in the background, by a well-known artist, which was to take pride of place above the mantelpiece, and elegant vases displayed seasonal flowers which added a touch of colour to the room.

The day the picture arrived I was standing in the lounge admiring it when the door opened behind me.

'Isn't it good?' I said to Nat, thinking it was she who was standing in the doorway.

When there was no reply I turned to find the big hairy form of Bongo staring at me. For a moment I stood transfixed while Bongo moved her attention from me to eye the new ornaments and decorations. Slowly she moved her 200-lb bulk into the room and began walking around to examine the new treasures more closely, casually picking them up and then dropping them on to the floor where, much to her satisfaction, they smashed into tiny pieces.

By this time, unknown to me, a call had gone out warning everyone to keep away from the area near the Gorilla House as somehow our stringent security precautions had gone awry and the gorillas had escaped. Nat and some of the keepers were already outside armed with chocolate bars to entice them back into the safety of the gorilla section. Their plan had worked perfectly and all the rest of the gorillas had returned to their quarters with the exception of Bongo, who had eaten all the chocolate bars and instead of heading for freedom had made her way to the house which had been her home for her formative years.

While Bongo was happily engrossed in the pleasurable pastime of trashing our newly acquired treasures, I slipped out of the room and shouted for help. By the time Nat came to my aid most of the ornaments were in pieces on the floor.

While staff were despatched to alert the vet, who fortunately was already on the premises, Nat went into the room with Bongo and began passing out what remained of our possessions to me through the window, one by one.

The vet arrived with a collar which Bongo allowed us to put round her neck, but when we tried to persuade her to move she flatly refused. There was no alternative but to use the tranquilliser pistol. The vet handed it to Nat, who took aim and Bongo collapsed in a crumpled heap. The sleeping gorilla was then heaved on to a stretcher and returned to join the rest of her mates in the Gorilla House, where no doubt she awoke thinking that it had all been a dream.

Thankfully that most dramatic of all our escapes has not been repeated.

CHAPTER NINETEEN

Vets' Advances

Over the years there have been startling improvements and breakthroughs in veterinary medicine which have saved the lives of sick and injured animals, and we have good reason to be grateful to our stalwart veterinary surgeons who have played a vital role in the success of Twycross Zoo.

Looking back, it is hard to believe the advances the veterinary profession and scientists have achieved. In the past there were fewer drugs and less knowledge. This applied to the medical profession too.

As a child both Nat, myself and other children of our generation had our tonsils removed by a GP on the kitchen table. I don't remember a thing about it, but Nat has vivid recollections of the doctor soaking cotton wool with chloroform in a gravy strainer before putting it over her face. In the same way, in the early days, if we needed to anaesthetise a monkey we had to do it by soaking some cotton wool with chloroform and waving it under its nose on a stick. Thank God those days are long gone and today both humans and animals benefit from the skill of doctors and vets and the sophisticated drugs they can offer.

One of the memorable cases at the zoo was when William, a young four-year-old chimp, got his leg tied up in a rope which was hanging from a bar. His two chimp companions alerted us to his plight by screaming and we arrived on the scene to find him hanging upside down in obvious pain while the other chimps, upset at his distress, were doing their best to free him by biting at the rope.

As soon as they saw us they realised that we had come to help and allowed us to move them away while one of us supported William's weight and the other cut him down with a knife. Once freed from the rope, we could see that William's leg was very swollen and we carried him over to the car and drove him back to the house.

The vet had already been alerted that there was an emergency and he arrived within twenty minutes. When he examined William's leg he suggested that the little chimp should be tranquillised and taken to his surgery for an X-ray. The verdict was that William had a broken leg; this was set in plaster while he was still under the anaesthetic before we returned to the zoo.

What do you do with a chimp with its leg in plaster? William obviously could not be put back with his friends just yet, so we decided that he would have to sleep in the house. A camp bed was put up in my bedroom, as it was vital that we kept a constant eye on him in case he tried to remove the plaster when he woke up. William was still soundly under sedation when we tucked him up into the camp bed, where he slept like a log.

In the morning he was a 'Hopalong Cassidy' but he soon learned that, although he was somewhat handicapped, he could manage to get about quite well. He lapped up all the sympathy and disrupted the whole household by stomping around and showing off.

After five days the plaster began to wear thin on his foot, due to his stamping it forcibly on the ground to attract attention. The vet came up with the idea of covering it over with fibreglass, which worked brilliantly – apart from the fact that we were all nearly overcome by fumes from the chemicals and it took such a long time to set that we had to take William for a car ride round and round the zoo to keep him occupied until the cast had hardened.

William thought it was all great fun! The fibreglass had to be changed fairly often, so on subsequent occasions we did it in the front porch with William sitting in a chair so that we did not suffer any ill-effects. He behaved impeccably, knowing that he was going for yet another ride. Six weeks is a long time to keep a chimp amused and remain sane. Often it was a battle of wills to keep the house looking like a home.

When the time came for the plaster to come off, he was very excited and so were we. As if understanding what was to happen, William sat very still despite the fact that he was nervous, but he was intrigued and watched carefully as the cast was cut off. When it was removed he gave a grunt of approval, rubbed his leg and then tugged us towards the door to let us know that he wanted to return to his mates, who greeted him like a longlost hero. The vet had prescribed plenty of exercise as physiotherapy and his friends certainly made sure he got plenty of that as they raced around the enclosure and wrestled with each other. Needless to say he made a complete recovery.

Another common problem with animals is their teeth; as with humans, they can decay and cause pain and swollen gums. In an animal the first indication is usually that it goes off its food, sometimes rubs its face and dribbles. If these warning signs are not picked up on early enough, the animal will begin to lose weight.

We had one old Colobus Monkey that once had to have eight teeth removed. Unlike humans, monkeys cannot be fitted with false teeth so they have to be fed finely chopped food until the gums harden.

When Joe the gorilla began holding the side of his face and was obviously in pain, our vet consulted a dentist who agreed to assist him when the extraction took place. An appointment was made for the following week and the dentist duly arrived with various dental implements that might be needed in the event of any complications.

He was visibly overawed by the size of his unusual patient but bravely stood by while our vet administered the tranquilliser with a blowpipe. After a few minutes, Joe gave a grunt and gently collapsed into oblivion. When he had been lifted on to the table, one of his large molars was extracted and the rest of his teeth were given a thorough examination by the dentist before a further injection brought him round from the sedation. When he recovered consciousness he looked like many dental patients, very sorry for himself, but took the drink he was offered. The next day the swelling had gone down and Joe was back to his usual boisterous self.

On another occasion it was our male lion who first of all became very bad-tempered and dribbled at the mouth. The vet decided that it was necessary to tranquillise him to investigate the cause. The anaesthetic was administered with a blowpipe containing a syringe filled with a sedative. Using a pipe instead of a tranquilliser gun is preferable because there is no loud noise when it is fired, and apart from the initial impact, it causes little distress and, as in the case of our lion, the patient is soon asleep.

When the vet examined the lion, it looked as though in addition to a bad tooth the jawbone could be infected, and so a blood sample was taken for testing and the lion was allowed to come round while we waited for the results to come back.

The jaw was certainly infected and four days later he was once more tranquillised while the vet not only removed a tooth but also part of the jaw. The lion made a good recovery but was left with a sore mouth and for several days was fed on minced meat and warm milk. After a week his temper had improved and in ten days he was back to normal.

In the old days the use of tranquillisers was very hit and miss. Today the sedatives are more refined and their effect far more predictable, which is vital when the animals being sedated are highly strung, like the giraffe. In fact, the whole operation of tranquillising one of these creatures needs to be far more precise than with less delicate animals. The great danger of sedating giraffes, is that because of the length of their necks, they must not be allowed to slump down; their head and neck must be propped upright, otherwise it can be fatal.

If any animal is off-colour, the first step is to send faeces and urine samples to the laboratory for testing, which results in many causes of illness being diagnosed and treated at an early stage.

Apes share many human illnesses and conditions; one of these is diabetes. One chimp in a Canadian zoo became so used to having her daily injection of insulin that she would come and helpfully present her rump at the bars. Apes are particularly aware that you are trying to help them when they are sick, and so they try to co-operate.

Some animals do suffer from heart problems that would have gone unnoticed in the old days. Today they undergo the same tests as we do and are given pills to alleviate the problem. How do we administer the pills? In jam on a spoon, of course!

The chimps we are very proud of having at Twycross are our rare Chocolate Chimps and it is one of these, Jambo, who has caused us a lot of heartache. Until a few years ago, Jambo was one of the most handsome chimps at the zoo, with a lovely, shiny chocolate coat. Then, for no apparent reason, within a week he lost all his hair. We sent for Roger, our vet, and Jambo was duly darted with a sedative so that he could be examined and tests carried out.

His skin, which had been covered by a fine crop of hair, was now dry and itchy, and whatever was causing the problem had destroyed the hair follicles. Roger did skin scrapings, blood tests and carried out a thorough examination before prescribing an all-over bath with an antibacterial shampoo and coating him with special cream.

Despite all our best efforts, two years later his skin condition still has not been cured, although Roger believes that Jambo is suffering from some kind of allergy which we have yet to pinpoint. It is notoriously difficult to specify particular allergies in humans; it is even more difficult in animals that cannot speak and so we continue with varying treatments in the hope that one day Jambo will be cured.

So far we have used creams and lotions recommended

by herbalists, dermatologists and homeopaths and have consulted experts from all over the world.

One herbal ointment appeared to be working and Jambo began to grow some new but fine hair, then our hopes were dashed. Although his condition improved, it was not cured and we still have to bathe him every two weeks and coat him with cream to keep his skin supple.

At the onset of his hair loss Jambo was very miserable and became very shy, as if he felt embarrassed about his baldness. Now he has totally accepted his problem and is so philosophical about his fortnightly baths that when Roger arrives he knows exactly what is going to happen and presents his rump so that the vet can tranquillise him. Our ongoing efforts may not have brought back his hair, but the bathing and the creams keep his skin smooth and at least he is not scratching.

Jambo is now so completely unperturbed by his odd looks that he has no hesitation in displaying his naked physique to the public as he rushes round his enclosure proudly displaying his all like a streaker! Some people have suggested that we have him put down, but I would never countenance that, not unless he was in constant pain. He will spend the rest of his life here at Twycross and may yet father some lovely Chocolate Chimp babies. In the meantime we can only hope that one day someone will find a magic cure that will restore him to his former glory.

There *are* magic remedies around – as we discovered when our precious Bonobos all went down with flu and were very hard hit by the virus. Conventional antibiotics seemed to have little effect so we put out a plea over the Internet asking if anyone could suggest any remedy. We had hundreds of calls, including one from a vet in Israel who arranged for us to be sent six bottles of herbal medicine which he insisted would help cure their condition.

Although we were sceptical, we felt that it was worth giving it a try and to our amazement, twenty-four hours after their first dose, their condition had improved dramatically.

On many occasions we have had the benefit of doctors and specialists, including paediatricians whose knowledge about human births and babies is easily related to our closest cousins, the apes. Consulted by our vets, they have been very happy to give their time and expertise to helping our animals, and on one occasion when one of our gorillas gave birth to a premature baby, a local hospital sent out qualified staff with an incubator and premature baby clothes, including a little woolly hat.

In spite of them doing everything possible, the baby died within twenty-four hours and the nurses from the Premature Baby Unit were very upset and said that if it had been possible to have taken the baby back to the hospital, they felt it might have survived.

Female gorillas like Bongo have undergone extensive tests including blood tests, vaginal probes and ultrasound to see if their ovaries are functioning properly. In Bongo's case, despite the fact that all her reproductive organs were found to be perfectly healthy, she never did conceive and produce her own baby. She has spent her life being happily fulfilled acting as aunt to the others.

We are very lucky in our vet as he and his partners are on twenty-four-hour call, and if a complicated operation has to be carried out at the zoo he brings one of their qualified veterinary nurses and an anaesthetist.

When Roger Coley took over from our vet Mary Brancker on her retirement, he volunteered to spend six months without pay assisting her so that he could learn from her wealth of experience about all the animals and the procedures. This generous act has stood him in good stead.

Now he makes regular weekly visits – but he never has to announce his arrival. The animals do it for him! It is like the bush telegraph: once one animal recognises him, they show their feelings by shaking their bars, yelling or throwing things at him as they remember the indignities they have suffered at his hands.

In winter we give our apes and monkeys additional

vitamins and minerals to boost their resistance to infection. Every morning I do the rounds of the chimps armed with a bottle of Haliborange and they love it so much that they queue up for their spoonful of tonic like children.

But it's not only the apes and monkeys that have to take avoiding action. Because the animals are so susceptible to catching viruses and influenza from their human contacts, we ask all the keepers who are their regular companions to have a flu jab at the beginning of the winter. Our local GP comes by appointment to the house to administer the injection to the keepers and we have found that it has been very successful in cutting down absences due to flu and cases of our animals being infected.

Why don't we give the animals the vaccine themselves? you may ask. The answer is that, in order to do so, they would all have to be tranquillised. Not really a viable option.

One of the most testing cases for our veterinary surgeon was when our magnificent Toucan managed to catch its long bill in the wire of the aviary and ripped the upper part right off. The only part of its upper beak that remained was a few inches that were attached to its jaw. Without a complete bill it was impossible for the bird to eat, so it was vital that we devise something that would take the place of the missing mandible.

In the end it was decided to make it a false upper bill out of fibreglass, which was easily attached to the remaining piece and was formed to look like the real thing. The trickiest part of the operation was giving the right amount of anaesthetic, as birds can have a bad reaction to it, but in this instance the whole operation went smoothly, the false bill was attached and the Toucan made an excellent recovery. He was able to use his new appendage as expertly as his missing one, and therefore avoided starvation. The fibreglass bill never had to be replaced and the Toucan lived to be a ripe old age.

CHAPTER TWENTY

Orphans in the House

Over the last thirty-seven years our house has welcomed a whole procession of orphans through its
door. More than twenty baby chimps and numerous other
apes and monkeys including orangs, gorillas, gibbons and
howler monkeys have shared our home and sometimes
our beds.

It isn't only orphan monkeys and primates that needed
to be hand-reared of course. During our time at Twycross
we have played nursemaid to an assortment of other baby
animals of all shapes and sizes. The one thing they had in
common was that their own mothers had rejected them
and that they needed special care and attention if they
were to survive.

Individual characters, diverse personalities – each of
them has left lasting memories of sleepless nights, getting
up for three-hourly feeds or changing nappies; of riotous
bath-times with the bathroom awash with water and foam,
and of anxious hours keeping vigil over a sick animal as it
fought for its life.

We had many disappointments and much heartache
when, despite all our efforts, a tiny animal died. These
were outweighed by the utter satisfaction of watching
baby animals mature and grow stronger until they were
well enough to take their place with companions of their
own kind in the zoo.

One of the more unusual characters to take up residence
in the house was Polly the parrot, who was left to us by a
wealthy lady in her will. Polly came with her own dowry,

a legacy that was to pay for her keep for as long as she lived. We agreed to take her in, and this well-off Green Amazon Parrot became known as 'Polly with the Lolly'.

Despite her deceased owner's generosity in making provision for her companion's future, Polly, being a long-lived bird, outlived her dowry but, I am glad to say, is still living in style with the rest of our parrots in the Bird House.

Polly's duration in the house was certainly the longest but not the most memorable. Of all the creatures we entertained in our home, a tiny Indian Otter cub called Totty certainly left her mark.

When we first bought a pair of smooth-coated Indian Otters we had great hopes that they would breed, but as time passed they showed no inclination to mate. We sought advice from Nicole Duplaix-Hall, who has devoted her life to the study of otters, and showed her the area we had provided for the otters, which was perfectly adequate but not very imaginative. It consisted of a small pool inside a concrete enclosure and, although the otters seemed quite happy, we had realised that it did not possess any features of the otters' natural habitat.

Following Nicole's recommendations, we designed an enclosure that would resemble as far as possible the natural habitat of these lovely creatures. We dug out a completely new, larger area, which had a thirty-feet pool with a waterfall and rockery, plus a dirt area where they could dig. The rest was turfed, and to make it more attractive to the public as well as otterproof, instead of using a wire-mesh barrier we dug out a moat and surrounded it with a wall. We also built the otters a house which was tiled and had underfloor central heating – everything an otter could wish for, in fact! We were very proud of the result and could not wait to introduce the couple to their new home.

Well, it may have been to *our* liking, but when we came out to view them the next morning, it seemed the otters had felt they could improve on it. They had been very busy during the night, and the result was the enclosure now looked like a shambles. The otters had rolled up all the turf like a carpet and had scattered bits of it all over the surface of the pool, which was now brown and muddied.

We were devastated at their adverse reception to our carefully thought-out improvement and had to put them into temporary quarters which by comparison looked like a slum, with an old galvanised bath and a wooden hut while we restored their new run to its former glory.

The pool was emptied and cleared of debris, the turf was pegged down so they could not remove it and they were once more returned to their new home. Oddly enough they made no more attempts to deface it and, to our delight, that September they decided to mate and two months later produced a beautiful female cub – the first Indian Otter cub to be born at the zoo, to add to our other successes.

Our exhilaration was soon replaced by a familiar sinking feeling as, having given birth, the female otter appeared to have no idea how to look after the cub. After twenty-four hours the cub was looking very blue and exhausted and we realised that she had not been fed. It was November and bitterly cold for any baby, and we knew that she needed food and warmth if she was to survive.

Reluctantly we made the decision to remove her from her mother and take her into the house. We had no idea then of the chaos one tiny otter cub would bring to our lives. Like kittens, otter cubs' eyes do not open for a month after they are born, but this did not stop her from constantly screaming for food and attention. We had always thought that gorillas and the other apes were exacting, but Totty beat them hands down.

Once her eyes were opened she would follow us everywhere. Before I could close the door on her she would be in the lounge, in the kitchen and into everything.

We had given her a box in the bathroom as her home, but if we dared to shut her in she would scratch the door with her long claws and scream until we gave in and let her out.

For months the smell of fish that was her staple diet permeated the house. The bathroom had seemed the most appropriate location, as it was important that even as a small cub Totty should learn to swim. First we held her gently in a few inches of water in the handbasin until she had mastered the technique, and then moved her into the big bath where her natural instincts soon took over.

She loved to play in the water, and we encouraged her to become more proficient by floating ping-pong balls on the water, which she would swim after and nudge along with her nose.

As she grew bigger she did give us a few frights. One day we went into the bathroom to find that Totty had disappeared. We panicked, because she was so quick and agile she could have slid through the door without us noticing and could be anywhere. We called her name and, before we could organise a major search, Totty's head popped up from the loo, where she had spotted water and decided to investigate. After that, if she ever disappeared she could usually be found in the toilet.

It became apparent that she could not stay in the house for ever, neither could she be returned to live with her parents, as Indian Otters live in pairs and they would have rejected her as an intruder.

In the end we decided to place her on deposit with Philip Ware of The Otter Trust in Norfolk, and for the first time in months the house was free of the smell of fish.

The following year our otters mated again and produced six cubs which were strong and healthy. After her first disastrous attempt as a mother, our female otter seemed to have developed strong maternal instincts and fed and cared for them with the help of the proud father who doted on his offspring.

All was well until the cubs were three months old, when the otters decided that it was time their babies learned to swim. Following the usual method of teaching a cub to survive in water, Mum carefully launched herself into the water with one of the cubs on her back.

Once in the middle of the pond she dived from under him, leaving the cub to thrash about in the water, somehow managing to reach the side and climb on to terra firma. Obviously disappointed with the cub's efforts, the mother picked him up and unceremoniously threw him back into the water. Then she and her mate joined the floundering cub as if to give him encouragement, ignoring the fact that the youngster kept disappearing underwater.

Each time the cub managed to get back to land, the mother threw him into the freezing cold water again. Meanwhile, the other cubs ventured one by one into the water, where they splashed around until they managed to swim while their luckless brother, totally exhausted, sank to the bottom of the pool.

Luckily for the cub, a photographer who had been taking pictures of these swimming lessons saw the cub's plight and rushed to fetch us. When we arrived, the cub was lying at the bottom of the pool. Nat immediately waded to the rescue, then proceeded to give the cub mouth-to-mouth resuscitation. It was not the first time or the last that Nat's prompt action had saved the life of an animal, and within minutes the cub began to breathe again and opened its eyes.

We rushed him back to the house and put him in hot water to bring his temperature to normal and then kept him warm for the rest of the day. We were determined that this time, if possible, he would be restored to his parents, and by night-time, when he had recovered completely, we reinstated him in the otter enclosure. His parents welcomed him back, but we took no chances and emptied the pool except for a few inches of water.

It was as well we did, for the next day they carried on their roles as swimming instructors, forcing the cub back into the remaining inches of cold water until, in desperation, we drained it off completely.

We could not leave the otters without any water so we compromised by giving them some in a bowl, whereupon they immediately picked up the protesting cub and dunked him in the water.

At our wits' end, we substituted a shallow tray for the bowl so that when the otters tossed the cub into this vessel it was only deep enough for him to paddle. Phew! Talk about sink or swim!

During all this time we had other houseguests that needed our attention. We achieved another first, when our Pileated Gibbon gave birth to the very first baby to be born in Britain; sadly, she immediately rejected it, leaving us to bring the tiny ape up in the house. After that, she produced another eight babies but refused to look after any of them for more than a few days.

Fortunately, over the years, we found willing foster parents in our Great Danes, male and female, who were very tolerant of all the orphans who invaded their territory, but seemed to take a particular liking to the gibbons and would allow them to snuggle up to them in front of the fire.

Perhaps it was because all of the dogs were rescued and this background might have given them an affinity to other animals that were in need of help.

Our first Great Dane, a magnificent black animal called Prince, had been trained for security work as a guard dog. The dog warden who brought him to us explained his background and, as he left, ordered Prince to 'stay'.

We went with the man to his car to see him off and when we returned to the lounge where we had left Prince, he growled and refused to let us in. He was protecting the premises. After many hours and much tempting with food, he decided to call a truce and allowed us to feed him. Eventually he settled into his new routine but would guard the premises and us diligently.

To strangers he could appear fierce, but when he was introduced to his very first baby gibbon his gentle nature shone out. Wimpy the Pileated Gibbon was taken under Prince's wing and it was heartwarming to see the tiny gibbon snuggling up to the huge dog, who was as gentle as a kitten.

He was equally tolerant of Joe the gorilla when he was a baby and would accept the rough horseplay and join in chasing the baby gorilla around the house. When Prince died, a succession of Great Danes showed the same caring attitude to all our orphans, including monkeys, chimps, otters, tapirs, even Polly the parrot – and were incredibly tolerant when they were tormented and teased by the cheekier youngsters.

The next dog, Brandy, came from a vicarage. When the rector had been taken ill, the dog was sent to the Great Dane Rescue to be rehomed. In his early days Brandy had had his spleen removed and from the time he came to us he was never a very healthy dog and died at the age of nine.

We were so impressed by the Great Dane Rescue that we returned there after he died, as we had been told that they had four Great Danes who needed rehoming. When we arrived at the kennels all the dogs were barking and it was pandemonium. One of the kennel maids went to fetch a fawn dog for us to look at and we watched as he dragged her all the way down the path.

I looked at Nat and knew that she was reacting exactly as I was, instantly deciding that he was a dog that we would not be able to manage, but when he came up to us and looked at us with his big, sad eyes, as if pleading for us to give him a chance, I relented. He was very thin and had obviously been fretting at the kennels.

'Give me his lead,' I told the girl and I walked him away from the kennels. For the first few steps he pulled, and then his pace slackened and he walked to heel. And so we took him home. We called our new Great Dane Coaley, because he had belonged to a coalman and had been his constant companion, sitting next to him on the front seat of the lorry while his owner made his calls. Business was bad and when the hard times came the coalman could no longer afford to keep his pet and had reluctantly sent him to the kennels to be rehomed. Coaley did indeed have the most wonderful temperament and soon settled in with Bugsy, our French Bulldog, and our other assorted guests.

At this time we were bringing up chimps in the house, and Coaley adored them. He would let them wrestle with him, he'd chase around after them and even when they teased him he never took offence. He would let them get away with murder.

Some of the most delicate monkeys were the Howler Monkeys from South America. The ones we had over the years from dealers arrived in such poor health that despite our best efforts they died. Then one Red Howler arrived in a consignment from Canada; small and sick, somehow he managed to survive, but he was never a healthy monkey.

We tried giving him multi-vitamins, vitamin B injections and protein supplements, but despite our ministrations he was never well enough to survive outside of the house. We decided that we would try to find him a companion and she arrived in the shape of a Black Howler Monkey. As she herself was suffering from dietary deficiencies and we could never stabilise her health, she was really the most compatible companion for him.

The couple lived in the house for years alongside our succession of Great Danes. Coaley joined in with all their games and would bark loudly and run down the stairs when the playful monkeys indulged in one of their favourite pastimes, sliding down the banisters.

When our star chimp Tina retired from Transatlantic races and her heady career as a film star, she mated, but to our great dismay the baby was stillborn. When she conceived again, Mary Brancker was concerned about the wellbeing of the baby as Tina was showing signs of toxaemia. She prescribed heart tablets and diuretics to help Tina through the pregnancy.

With no means of knowing the date of conception, we were completely taken by surprise when we went into Tina's cage one morning to find what looked like a tiny doll lying on a shelf in the bed quarters. The only sign of life was a tiny movement of the little chimp's diaphragm. I knew that we only had minutes to remove the baby if we were to have any chance of saving its life. I also knew that although Tina was showing no interest, she would not let me remove it. I had to tempt her away with a drink and then rush over to shut the sliding door between us and grab the baby.

Once again back at the house it was Nat who gave the pathetic little mite mouth-to-mouth resuscitation and brought it round. Fortunately, Mary Brancker was paying a visit to another sick animal at the zoo when a few hours later the baby chimp stopped breathing. An injection of heart stimulant revived her, but we had no confidence that she would survive as she weighed only twenty-four ounces, just half the normal weight of a newly born chimp.

We had not reckoned with the little one's fighting spirit and despite all her problems she began to improve. She slept in a cage in Nat's bedroom so that we could take turns to feed her at three-hourly intervals, and gradually she began to gain weight.

At three weeks old she caught a cold and had to be put into an oxygen tent for a month. Now we were really convinced that we would lose her. It was only her indomitable spirit that helped her fight her way back to health.

Rosie, as we called her, was never strong and tired very easily when she played with the other chimps. Instinctively I knew that something drastic was wrong and called in Mary Brancker, who examined her and confirmed my suspicions that Rosie had a heart condition. The good news was that it could be kept under control by medication.

Rosie became one of the more long-term residents in the house and was joined for a time by three other chimps, Louis, Kip and Jill – all of whom needed special attention.

With so many babies crammed into our home and the prospect of more baby apes and monkeys in the future, we decided to build an ape nursery in the zoo with a heated indoor playroom equipped with nursery furniture, climbing frames, slides and plastic barrels. The little ones could play there in any weather and it provided another attraction for the public, who loved to watch the babies romping around.

As if to compensate for her poor health, Rosie was an extremely clever chimp who needed to have new challenges to keep her amused. She quickly learned how to turn on the radio and tune in to her favourite programmes, loved watching television and when she was tired would put herself to bed, arranging the pillows and blankets to her liking.

Having vowed I would never toilet train another chimp after Sue, because they usually want to go at the most inconvenient moments, I relented and within days Rosie had grasped what was required. I should have known better. It became an obsession with her and even if I put her in nappies at night she would wake up and blow raspberries at me until I prised my eyes open and took her to the toilet. Invariably when we came back to bed, after she had carefully flushed the loo, she would immediately fall asleep while I remained wide-awake listening to her contented snores.

Rosie was so accustomed to her routine that if Nat and I were both away at once, one of the keepers had to sleep with her to keep her company – and escort her for her nightly visits to the loo.

Eventually we found a suitable friend for Rosie and she moved out into the zoo.

We were not long without another, far different, infant taking up residence in her place. We had waited ten long years hoping that our precious Malayan Tapirs would breed and had almost given up the idea when their keeper came running to tell us that he had found a newly born baby in the straw in their house.

Sure enough, there was a tiny, squat black baby covered with the distinctive spots and stripes which act as camouflage to protect the tapirs from predators while they are young. Later, as they mature, these fade and the animal will develop the black and white uniform of its parents.

The newly born tapir seemed contented enough, but when we returned three hours later it was still lying in the same position away from its parents. We gave them a feed to distract them while we examined the baby more closely. There seemed nothing visibly wrong with her, except she could not stand. We consulted Mary Brancker, who was convinced that the tapir was suffering from the same condition that affects some foals. If her diagnosis was correct, the good news was that, like foals, the tapir would grow out of it.

We kept the baby warm by putting her into a straw-filled box under an infra-red lamp, the kind used to rear baby chicks. Fed with goat's milk and kept warm like this, at the end of a week she was already trying to stand. By now she had grown fatter, and to me her body looked too heavy for her legs to be able to support it.

We bandaged her front legs to give her more support and watched despairingly as she still staggered about and regularly fell over. We had no intention of giving up; our baby tapir was too precious, and after fourteen weeks we were rewarded when she could support her 50 lb weight and walk quite normally.

The young tapir was the first nocturnal animal we had kept in the house. She would sleep for most of the day and then, most disconcertingly, would start trundling about the house during the night. As soon as she was old enough in the spring she was able to take up residence in a paddock next to her parents.

Not long after she moved out, Coaley died at the age of eight from an infection. It was a blow to us. Despite the efforts of a vet, and specialist treatment, we were unable to save him. Poor Coaley. Once again we looked for a rescue dog who needed a good home and found a large black Great Dane called Duke. He had already had five homes and had gained the reputation of being a problem dog.

The woman who had offered him his fifth home – a council house which he shared with her large family and two Rottweilers – said she was parting with him because she could not exercise him. None of them could control him on a lead.

The manager of the rescue kennels admitted that they had taken Duke on condition that should they not find a suitable home for him, he would have to be put down. For once it was me who was cautious and Nat who let her heart rule her head. She said that on no account could we let him be put down; we would take him. The next day when we collected Duke we found that his last owner was quite right; we couldn't manage him on a lead either – *he* managed us.

The only solution was to buy a 'Halti' – a kind of head-collar that will turn the dog's head if you pull on the lead, making him go round in a circle. Having solved one problem, we almost immediately met with another, for the next day Duke bit one of our staff. He obviously could not be trusted with other people. Still, Nat and I decided to persevere and within the next two weeks he gained weight, learned to walk on a lead and, apart from his temperament, was a great dog. Whatever grudges he held against humans, he was totally loyal to his new friend Bugsy, our French Bulldog, and to any of the orphans with whom he came into contact. It was humans, not other animals, that had let him down.

Duke died after two years from a suspected tumour on the brain. At least after a chequered start he had enjoyed that short period of care and affection.

Now we have a two-year-old bitch, another Great Dane, from the Canine Defence League, who are doing a wonderful job rescuing and rehoming dogs of all breeds. Her name is Taz, and she is a well-trained gentle giant who has decided that she will sleep with one of us at night and occupy the large settee in the sitting room by day. She also tried to play with Bugsy, who is now nearly ten years old and frowns upon such antics.

Although she had never before been in contact with any of the strange-looking orphans she has encountered since she arrived here, Taz has taken it all in her stride.

Our latest chimp to be hand-reared is Danny, who is now three years old and has made the transition from the house to the ape nursery but still retains his loving sociable ways.

Taz always gives him a great welcome when he comes back to the house to do a photo session or meet guests. She has also taken a great interest in the Zebu calf which we have in the house to hand rear after its mother rejected and which needs feeding every four hours. Zebu cattle are the sacred cows of India with a small hump behind their necks, and Taz is far closer to their size than the tiny calf she wants to play with.

Nat and I also have two cats, the feral kind, who adopted us and have their own shed in the outside yard where they are fed daily. Last year we could not understand why they were eating such a lot and only visiting the shed very briefly, when they would lie right at the back of it instead of in the deep bed of shredded paper which we provided for them to make their nest.

When we investigated by lifting the paper we discovered that a hedgehog had taken up residence and had given birth to a litter of five babies. There they were hidden under the paper, tiny little pink bodies with very soft prickles. They stayed there for six weeks sharing the residence with the two cats until one night they disappeared. Mum must have decided they were old enough to walk and follow her to pastures new in the zoo where she would teach them to forage for their own food. Perhaps she will return this year to have another family. We certainly hope so.

At the moment, gardeners are very busy planting trees and shrubs, bees are at work in the flowerbeds and butterflies are settling on the buddleia

The hedges, which go right round the boundary of the zoo, have to be cut twice a year, but we never do it in spring when the birds are nesting. So many hedgerows throughout the countryside have been dug up, depriving wildlife of its natural habitat. Our hedges are kept safe for sparrows, starlings, thrushes and finches and we are rewarded when we see the young birds just out of the nest learning to fly. And in the autumn the same hedges will be abundant with blackberries and hawthorn berries for them to live off.

With the exception of the Zebu calf, the house for once is free of orphans, but not for long. Spring is a time for giving birth. We have already had the great news that the Barbirusa has given birth to twins; the Black and White Ruffled Lemurs have had a baby and the Sand Cats have produced a litter of four kittens; at the moment, mothers and babies are doing fine.

But no doubt over the next months there will be other babies who will need tender, loving care and once more the house will come to life with the patter of tiny paws and endless sleepless nights.

CHAPTER TWENTY-ONE

The Zoo at Christmas

When we were approached by the BBC in 1998 asking if we would allow them to film a television series about our primates, we were very pleased that they had chosen Twycross.

The programme was to be called *Molly's Zoo*, which I must admit I did not like because I felt it was too personalised, but the fact that they wanted to film our apes – chimps, gorillas, orangs, Bonobos and gibbons – persuaded me.

The programmes would be filmed over a period of a year. I liked the producer John Hayes Fisher and his team immediately; not only were they considerate to me but they had an instant affinity with the chimps. At the end of each bout of filming I was interviewed in our lounge, which seemed very natural and informal. I think the fact that there was no pressure put on any of us, including the chimps, made the end result a success. Of all the filming I had done over the years, this was certainly the most enjoyable.

Two chimps were used during the programme – the young chimp called Danny, the son of Flynn and Becky, who must have inherited his kind nature from his parents; and another little chimp, Tommy, who while being devoted to me and very bright was also wilful and unpredictable.

At two years old he had had his front teeth knocked out in a brawl – which *he* had instigated – with another chimp, and when he smiled, showed 'nowt but gums'.

During filming, Danny travelled miles and miles driving round the zoo in my little car, with a cameraman in the back seat filming our progress. He absolutely adored every minute. Sometimes it was just Danny and me with a camera fitted to the front windscreen. The only problem was that when the producer told me to look into the camera I totally forgot about things like walls, and by the time the filming was over my poor old car was bruised and battered.

Chimps with different skills took part in some other scenes. Flynn was filmed as an artist, even though he is not as good as Joli, who was a little too unreliable to be filmed. She had definite artistic talent and had showed off her painting skills to David Shepherd when he paid us a visit. He was very impressed with her and added the finishing touches to her painting.

Filming the TV series produced some hysterically funny scenes, 'takeouts' which were never shown on camera. This occurred particularly during the filming of the Christmas programme, when two of the keepers went shopping for presents for the chimps. The local shopkeepers did not understand what they wanted with numerous plastic bowls, scrubbing brushes and furry toys. They didn't realise that chimps adore nothing better than to be given a bucket of water and a cloth, and will spend hours washing their enclosures. With all the aplomb of an experienced window cleaner they will carefully wring out the cloth before washing the windows of their quarters. The keepers are not so keen on this activity and watch with horror while their beautifully shiny glass is turned into a smeared mess by the chimps' enthusiastic efforts.

The programme also showed one of the staff going to a local garden centre to purchase a ten-foot Christmas tree. When it arrived it was tied in a net and very bulky, so much so that we had great difficulty in manoeuvring it into the hall, where it was placed in a large pot and stabilised.

'What do we need a ten-foot Christmas tree for?' I innocently asked.

'So that the chimps can dress it with lights and baubles,' I was told.

Hmm. I could have warned them it would not be that simple, and I was right. Danny was in the scene with our French Bulldog Bugsy who, following the producer's wishes, had sat down obligingly under the tree. Everything was fine, except that instead of handing the trimmings to Nat, Danny insisted on showing them to Bugsy first. Even when he did hand them to Nathalie he would gaze at her effort and then demand that they should be moved because they were not to his liking.

It takes a very long time to film a Christmas-tree-trimming scene; the lighting has to be right, the chimp's expression has to be right and the dog has to be in the right place at the right time. Co-ordinating all these things was no easy task and the filming took hours. In fact, nothing would have been achieved without the tremendous co-operation of the keepers, who put in every effort to make the film a success, fitting in at odd times between their duties to suit the sequence of filming.

One of the shots was filmed at night. Lights were put on at the rear windows of the house and cameras were trained on Julie the Orang Keeper walking across our lawn on her way to check the orang who was about to give birth.

The lengths the team went to in order to achieve the effects they wanted showed a high degree of pro-fessionalism. As, when shooting a Christmas scene, they prayed for snow but day after day passed with not even one snowflake. Then one day, when they were filming something entirely different, there was a brief snowstorm and they all disappeared to film with great precision the few snowflakes falling outside. It made their day!

Another time they spent hours filming a large puddle on which they had sprinkled petals. I was never sure what this was for, and it was never shown in the programmes.

Although it was tiring at times, the cameraman, lighting technician, researcher, director and producer were always very patient and considerate, even when things did not go according to plan.

A gibbon who was hand-reared was filmed in the children's adventure playground, swinging on ropes and coming down the slide. She certainly enjoyed it and will probably remember this as one of the happiest days of her life. The chimps who took part were also pleased to have an interesting diversion from their usual routine, and the Bonobos certainly played to the cameras; but the gorillas starred in the most dramatic part of the programmes when they were filmed being tranquillised and transported to the new Gorilla House. The camera recorded their delight, once they had recovered from the trauma, with their new abode.

Off-camera, the episode which gave the crew and Nat the most laughs was the time I went in with Jomar and Vicky to be filmed giving each of them their morning tea. Turning to go, I discovered that in the excitement I had locked the inside door and lost the keys. My security-conscious habit of making sure the chimps were securely locked in backfired, and I was locked in too.

The two chimps were puzzled by my long stay in their territory but made me welcome and seemed to think it was a huge joke. I wasn't quite so amused and wondered how anyone could get me out, as their sleeping quarters are divided into two with a partition down the centre, and a sliding door which was locked and could only be operated from the indoor passage. Without a key to the inside door I was in a very precarious situation.

Nat set off to look for duplicate keys and eventually returned accompanied by the cameraman, with a set of keys to the outside enclosure. They managed to undo the padlock on the outside sliding door and lift the plastic flap that hangs over the outlet to prevent cold air getting into the chimps' bedplaces during severe weather.

It was Nat who then crawled through the aperture and handed me the keys through the central partition so that I was able to unlock the inside door and get free. It had delayed filming for well over an hour but everyone except me thought it a huge joke. I was definitely not amused!

The painstaking work that the BBC crew put in paid off. After the first programme appeared we received over eighty letters in five days from viewers congratulating us on our work with primates. When the other programmes were shown, people from all over the country came to see the main stars – the chimps, gorillas, orangs and gibbons. Every time I drove around the zoo, parents and children waved to me and would come up to say how much they had enjoyed their visit to Twycross. For the first time I had an idea what it must feel like to be a celebrity.

The real stars of the programmes, the animals, enjoyed being the centre of attention as the number of visitors increased tremendously. Thanks to the popularity of *Molly's Zoo* the numbers continued to increase, not only through the summer months but well into the winter, which was very gratifying for us and the animals. Usually as the misty, damp November days set in, visitors drop off and a blanket of quiet begins to settle over the zoo.

It is too cold for many of the animals to venture out of their heated quarters and it is now that the keepers need all their ingenuity to keep their charges from the onset of boredom. It is absolutely essential that primates in particular have play equipment, swings and ropes, which more recently have been replaced with fire hose – the kind used by the fire brigade – which does not fray and is more durable.

All primates love brightly coloured balls, but with some of the chimps the life expectancy of a ball is two days at the most before they manage to burst it. They then treat the fragmented pieces like collectors' items, carefully gathering them up and placing them in any container they can find in their runs. Over the next weeks these collectibles gradually become valueless junk as they go on to better things.

The chimps and Bonobos love the old clothes that the keepers distribute. Jumpers are their favourites, the

gaudier the colour the better, although it is not unusual to
see a chimp in a blouse or a pair of frilly pants. When they
get tired they gather their clothes up and carry them to a
quiet corner to build a nest in which they curl up for a
quiet siesta.

One very old chimp loves mirrors and carries a com-
puter disc in the groin of her leg, periodically pulling it out
to look at her reflection and going through a whole gamut
of expressions; pouting, pulling one eye down with her
finger and putting her tongue out.

Little things can give chimps a lot of fun; washing-up
bowls, water and a cloth will keep them occupied for ages,
splashing each other, wringing out the cloth and flicking at
each other.

Like us, they have particular likes and dislikes. They
squabble, they laugh and can get very upset when they fall
out with each other, and often when the screaming is over
the victor will go and gently put his arm around the
vanquished chimp as if to say, 'Let's be friends.'

Unless you have studied our nearest relatives as we
have, you cannot appreciate the depth of feeling and
emotions of which they are capable. Like human parents,
when their young are old enough, they teach them to walk
by standing in front of them, holding out their arms to
encourage them to take their first tentative steps. They care
for them when they are hurt or upset and correct them
when they are naughty and disobedient.

Their greatest entertainment definitely comes from the
zoo visitors. As far as they are concerned, the public come
in to amuse *them* – not the other way round. In summer
they see lots of people, which keeps them interested, but
in winter when there are fewer visitors they miss the
contact. They spend a lot of time looking out for the cars,
often from a vantage point at the top of one of the trees in
their enclosures, and are obviously disappointed when
only a few turn up.

The staff do their best to make up for this by giving them
extra food treats. Most of the food for the animals comes

from local markets. In addition, four times a week we send vans to collect fruit and vegetables from Safeway, usually coming up to, or past their sell-by date, which would otherwise be thrown away. This can include apples, oranges, coconuts, mangoes and bananas; and on one occasion even toffee apples, which went down a treat with the chimps.

There is also an abundance of bread, cakes and biscuits and, as Christmas approaches, mince pies. All this is divided between all the sections so that everyone gets an equal share.

Ordinary tourist attractions, like theme parks, close their doors at the end of the season, but the zoo goes on all the time. The animals have to be cared for, cleaned, fed and amused 365 days of the year. Running a zoo in winter is a costly business, as temperatures still have to be maintained and heating costs soar to £16,000 a month.

The only day we close is Christmas Day, when the quietness of the zoo seems unreal. The animals know that it is different; they can sense it and would become very subdued if we did not make it a festive time for them with presents and special food treats. The chimps don't like the hush, they enjoy hustle and bustle and plenty of activity. That's why we make such a point of giving them Christmas presents to relieve the monotony,

The keepers will go and shop for presents and wrap them in colourful gift wraps. The gifts have to be one hundred per cent safe, which means that soft toys, which they destroy in minutes, and mechanical toys are out.

Instead, they will get plastic baby toys; plastic pegs which can be hammered into holes with a plastic hammer; plastic shapes; trains to pull along the floor and books suitable for one- and two-year-olds with colourful pictures.

Betty and Marcus, the Bonobo keepers, make their Christmas memorable by putting up decorations. As soon as the animals see the tinsel they get very excited. The wrapped presents are put into pillow-cases and placed on the Bonobos' shelves before they are let into their day quarters. When they scamper in and look around to see where the presents are, it is just like watching children on Christmas morning who can't wait to see what Father Christmas has brought. They are just as impatient to tear off the wrappings as any young child; their faces light up as they examine their gifts, especially the treats like avocados and mangoes, nuts and crisps which they find at the bottom of their pillow-case. Actually they enjoy undoing the parcel more than getting the presents!

Betty explains the emotions of most of the keepers: 'Christmas is a time to spend with your family. The Bonobos are my family and that's why I spend it here with them.

It's fun for them and for me. It's a very special time away from the public gaze, just between the keepers and the animals, a very personal celebration. They can have mangoes for breakfast and pig out on pop and crisps like any young kids.'

Other keepers give their animals different treats. Some of the hand-reared gibbons are taken by their keepers, Carol and Elaine, to the playground so that they can spend some time on the climbing frames and sliding down the chutes.

I usually give our gorillas, including Joe and Bongo, a box of ticket rolls. They love to undo them and throw them around and drape themselves with the tickets. It's very funny to watch and keeps them absorbed for hours.

Our youngest hand-reared chimp, Danny, joins us at the house to open his presents and have Christmas dinner at the table. He loves to watch television, and when he was younger his favourite programme was *The Teletubbies*, so he was delighted when he opened his presents to find his very own Teletubby doll, Laa Laa. When we took Danny back to his quarters at the end of the evening he went happily to bed clutching Laa Laa to him. After that he would never go anywhere without her.

Although we have reared so many baby chimps, Danny has won a special place in our hearts and with the public.

We do have many requests from children and adults to meet a chimp and although we can't always comply, we endeavour to respond to those who are handicapped or sick.

Danny is the obvious choice, as he is very sociable and safe, and he has brought a lot of pleasure to his 'patients', many of whom are in wheelchairs or on crutches. He has also met a lot of children who are blind and who have got a tremendous thrill out of feeling the texture of his face and ears and holding his hand – things that we sighted people take for granted.

One particular family came into our lives when they knocked on the door to ask if their little boy, who was terminally ill with leukaemia, could meet one of our chimps. It was a request we could not refuse and that day their son met Danny for the first time. It was an amazing meeting between the little boy and the young chimp. The boy's delight and Danny's instant empathy with him was very emotional for us and his parents.

This was the first of many visits over the next two years. Then, tragically, the boy's condition worsened and he was eventually taken into a local hospice. Knowing that he was dying, his parents made a special request. Would we take Danny to visit him?

When Danny arrived at the hospice and entered the ward he looked round and unhesitatingly went straight up to his sick friend, sat on his bed and put his arms around the little lad and hugged him. No words were exchanged; we just looked on and the expression on the boy's face and the rapport between the two was obvious to all of us standing around. I think we all had tears in our eyes.

Danny visited him once more and in some uncanny way seemed to understand how ill his friend was; he cuddled the lad as if to comfort him. Sadly it was the last time Danny would see his friend, for the little boy died the following day, but we were so glad that he had been able to make his last days happy.

CHAPTER TWENTY-TWO

Tomorrow's World

When we first entered the zoological arena, 'genes' meant a pair of blue denim trousers, 'gasp' was an exclamation of surprise, 'camp' was a place you went on holiday and a 'pair' of animals meant two of the same kind.

Now there is a scientific approach to breeding and genes are studied so that animals can be genetically paired, perfectly matched to produce Super-offspring; although, like us, unless they are compatible the end result is not always achieved.

And in zoological terms GASP is an abbreviation for Global Animal Survival Plan and CAMP stands for Conservation Assessment and Management Plan.

Conservation has been the theme of most zoological collections in the past, but without education we cannot begin to understand just how important conservation is for the future of our planet.

How many people truly realise what is happening in the wild? How aware are we of the slash and burn policy that threatens the forests; the intrusion of logging and the inroads being made into natural habitat as jungle is being turned into farmland. It is a sad fact that we are felling trees at such a rapid rate that the forests and woodland can no longer support a viable animal population. This is happening all over the world and, tragically, future generations will only be able to see many of these animals in zoological collections.

We humans are responsible for the extinction of many species that once roamed freely. Many more continue to be threatened by large-scale poaching – for ivory, for tiger bones and for bushmeat. In the wild, all animals have natural predators who will attack and kill their prey for food or in some instances to establish dominance. They also face natural dangers like floods and famine, earthquakes and tornadoes, which all add to the threat to their survival.

But today Man is the worst predator, with rifles, traps and snares. Often animals are not even killed outright but are left wounded to die in agony or are maimed for life in a trap or snare.

If Man is hungry and hunts for food, perhaps this can be justified – but if it is to sell an animal as a trophy, as bushmeat to restaurants, or for the cruel satisfaction of killing one of God's creatures, how can this be countenanced? We all have to survive, but not at the expense and suffering of animals. They are part of our heritage and we are responsible for their future.

Attitudes must change and it is only by educating new generations who visit our zoo that we can convey to them the importance of preserving and maintaining what is left of the wild. Visits by schools, educational talks, labelling and graphics all help to spread the message *Survival of the Wild*.

At Twycross we do not only talk of animals but of fauna and flora; different climatic conditions and natural vegetation that must be nurtured and respected.

Most animals in zoos have been bred in captivity and have no memories of their natural habitats, but each and every one of them has the same requirements that they would have in the wild. And each and every species differs in the types of accommodation, temperature and diet they need if they are to thrive. As well as having varying needs, their temperaments vary too.

Many zoo animals have become domesticated and have acclimatised and adapted very well to their captive surroundings, but like us they need variety in their lives to keep them from being bored. It is up to their keepers to keep them constantly interested and give them the care and attention they need. Anyone who works with animals knows that not a day passes without learning something from their behaviour.

Looking after and caring for animals is a vocation not to be undertaken lightly. If we can also improve their future by scientific research and education, we will have made a valuable contribution to a better world.

In the early days, our keepers seemed to have a vocation and be dedicated. They often came from a farming background and had a great understanding and love of animals. Many of our staff in those days left to get married and have a family, but as soon as the children were of school age they came back to work at the zoo. Their experience has been invaluable in training younger staff, many of whom start under their schools' work experience schemes and like it so much they want to make it their career.

These days, in order to qualify as a zoo keeper, staff have to take a two-year City and Guilds Diploma Course in Animal Management. This includes practical work at the zoo with time off during working hours to study hygiene, animal health and husbandry, and all about the varying diets of the animals and birds. The latter is quite a wide subject, from the jumbo meals of elephants who are the biggest eaters to the minute menu of mynah birds.

Every day keepers chop fruit, thaw fish and mix multivitamin powders in order to satisfy the appetites of a thousand animals with different diets, tastes and food preferences. From grocery vans delivering vegetables to earthworm tubs arriving in the post, the food keeps coming and costs about £140,000 a year.

In the wild, gorillas munch their way through large quantities of leaves, fruit and shoots. Here at the zoo they eat lots of fruit and vegetables and then browse around their outdoor enclosures looking for a treat of sunflower seeds which have been scattered for them by the keepers.

Filtered shrimps are on the menu for flamingos. Bending

like Sherlock Holmes' pipe, their beaks are nature's finest filters. Their tongue acts as a piston, pushing water through lamellae at the side of the bill. This leaves a mouthful of small shrimp-like animals or algae for the flamingo to swallow.

At Twycross the flamingos eat their own kind of convenience food – BP Flamingo Pellets, which provide an all-purpose diet and even contain a chemical obtained from shrimps in the wild, sometimes substituted with the Red Robin colour feed that is responsible for their pink plumage.

In the wild, lions rest for most of the day, for sometimes up to twenty hours. When they fancy a light lunch of deer or jungle fowl, the females of the pride get together for a spot of co-operative hunting. Afterwards the male butts in for the 'Lion's Share' of the kill.

Lions will eat up to forty kilos of food in a single session, including organs like the guts and stomach contents of their prey. When they can get them, large meals are the order of the day, eaten two or three times a week.

At Twycross the lions and tigers are fed daily on mixtures of muscle meat plus bonemeal and vitamins. As in the wild, they are fed in the early evening, with the exception of one fast day a week to give their digestive systems a rest.

Foraging for food occupies much of a monkey's time in the wild and at Twycross we feed most monkeys four times a day. In between larger feeds, seeds, nuts and insects are scattered around some enclosures for the animals to find.

Such a large variety of diets makes for a lot of studying for the trainee keeper, in addition to which at the end of their course they have to do a written project on the animal of their choice. Their animal husbandry is assessed for the practical work they do at the zoo and they have to sit an exam after two years to become a qualified keeper.

Some people have a special intuition about animals and,

although they may not be academically brilliant, have that certain rapport that no amount of study can give you.

We always explain to new recruits that looking after animals is a vocation and that animals have to be fed every day, even at weekends and Bank Holidays. They are totally dependent on their keeper, unlike a factory machine which can be covered up and left with the loss of just a couple of days' production. So unless keepers are genuinely sick we do not expect them to take days off.

Zoos and keepers now have the benefit of the vast progress made in veterinary treatment. Today, many previously incurable diseases can now be treated; with X-ray equipment and modern sedation, broken bones, which in the past might have resulted in an animal being destroyed, can now be set and the animal lead a perfectly normal, active life.

Prior to the 1960s, when import and export controls were put in place, animals were subjected to appalling travelling conditions. Most were brought over by boat and were in transit for weeks, suffering changes of climate and lack of proper food or care. Today they travel by air, with a veterinary surgeon or a qualified animal keeper in attendance. Rules and regulations relating to the transportation of animals are strictly enforced. Crates or travelling boxes must comply with the regulations drawn up by the International Animals' Transport Authority (IATA) for the animals' welfare.

On long journeys animals are only allowed to travel for a set number of hours before having a period of rest – a stopover where they can be watered and fed. On arrival at their destinations they undergo inspection by a Ministry vet and are then sent to spend the required number of months in licensed quarantine quarters.

Twycross has always specialised in primates and has breeding groups of many species. Our Black and White Colobus Monkeys have produced a record seventy-five offspring over the years. These have been sent all over the world to form breeding groups in other zoological collections as far afield as Australia.

In the year 2000 we have sent animals to France, Germany, Budapest and Qatar. In return we have received animals from San Francisco, Prague and Mulhouse. By exchanging animals on breeding loan programmes we are helping to conserve many animals from the wild.

'What of the future?' you may ask.

With the help of all of you who read this, there can be hope that some of the animals throughout the world will once again survive and breed in their natural habitats protected from predators and poachers by dedicated rangers.

You can make a difference. You can make donations to wildlife trusts and you can spread the word. Start with your own children or grandchildren. Introduce them at an early age to the beauty of Nature around them. Teach them about the animals in the wild and the importance of wildlife.

As they grow older, make them aware of the results of global warming and how we are responsible, often through greed or ignorance, for destroying our own heritage. Teach them to conserve energy and make sure they learn about British wildlife and flora.

Spare a little time to take them out into the countryside. Observing the wonder and delight of a child discovering the joys of Nature is one of the most rewarding parts of education. Television is a wonderful medium, but you cannot experience from it the distinctive odours of animals or the heady scent of flowers. No matter how big the television screen, you do not get a true idea of the size of animals and birds in real life.

Many people bring children for a picnic at Twycross; some just have a bag of simple sandwiches and sit on the grass; others arrive with their own collapsible table and chairs, bottles of wine, fresh strawberries and exotic salads. The sound of the gibbons whooping, the sight of the orangs sitting under a blanket at the top of one of the trees in their enclosure, and the vivid pink shade of the flamingos paddling in their pool make it a perfect setting on a summer's day.

Over the years we have watched the evolution of our young visitors. They make their first visit to the zoo as toddlers with their family. By the time they are in their teens their interest in animals is overtaken by the thrills of white-knuckle rides and theme parks. When they are in their mid-twenties they come back with their own children, introducing a new generation to creatures from a different world; continuing the family interest in wildlife and conservation.

To keep the youngsters entertained in the early days, we installed a simple play area with swings, slides and see-saws. Now that children have become more sophisticated we have added an Adventure Playground which is divided into two sections; one for younger children aged up to six years old, the other for children up to fourteen (although it is not unusual to see fathers having a go on the 'Gorilla Reach' or the climbing frames!).

We also have a train that goes round the playground from which the children can see Cameroon Sheep, Alpacas and Zebu Cattle or have a ride on a donkey.

At Twycross we also run an active educational pro-gramme for schools who bring pupils on day trips here. Groups of Scouts, Brownies and Girl Guides make annual visits to study for their badges; students and teenagers taking part in the Duke of Edinburgh's Award Scheme come at weekends and school holidays to work with the animals, which not only helps them gain their diploma but gives them a lasting insight into wild animals. I hope that they will benefit from this contact as much as we have done.

My life over the past fifty years has been involved with chimps. They were the founder members of our collection and without their contribution there would never have been a zoo. I have been privileged to have worked with them and have brought many of them up as babies. I hope that Nat and I have improved the life of chimps who came to us from various backgrounds, many of them rescued from appalling conditions.

By turning Twycross into a charitable trust we have ensured their future. It was in 1972 that we made this decision. Neither Nat nor I had any human dependants; the only beings totally reliant on us were our animals, and we were determined that the zoo should remain their home, otherwise our lifetime's work would have been wasted.

The decision entailed us virtually relinquishing ownership of everything we had worked for. In the beginning we kept the land in our names until we were sure that this new arrangement would work, then we made it over to the trust.

Twycross Zoo officially became the East Midlands Zoological Society in 1972; a charitable trust which is managed by a council of members. Now we work for the charity. Apart from that, nothing has changed: it is still, and always will be, the animals who come first.

Our lives have been unimaginably enriched by the chimps and many other animals in our care, and I hope that we have managed to reciprocate a little by helping both animals in the wild and those in captivity.

All animals are individuals and should be treated as such, but our nearest relatives, the chimps, have given us a lifelong friendship that few will understand.

The animals in our care are ambassadors for animals in the wild and are playing their part in making visitors aware of the needs of those that remain in their natural habitat.

We are extremely lucky, over the years, to have had a very dedicated staff who we hope will follow in our footsteps and carry on our work in the future.

Afterword

Since the publication of *Molly's Zoo,* an outbreak of foot and mouth disease devastated the British farming industry and had a disastrous effect on tourism. Twycross was one of forty-two zoos closed for periods varying from three weeks to two months. No one could envisage the long-term effects it has had on the leisure industry.

In the case of Molly's Zoo, the gates remained closed for three weeks. Barriers of disinfectant were laid across all of the entrances and foot dips installed in strategic places. All vehicles coming into the Zoo had to be sprayed and the staff dip their shoes before entering the gates. Milk and stores were unloaded outside the main gates. Although the Zoo was not in quarantine, there were several outbreaks within a seven-mile radius.

The animals missed the public and sensed that there was something seriously wrong. The gibbons who usually greet the dawn remained silent. The chimps were despondent. The staff rallied round to entertain them and after a week the animals relaxed a little but a sense of cheerlessness still permeated the whole atmosphere. Molly was interviewed by reporters over the main entrance gate and she asked them if they noticed anything different. They said yes, the deathly silence and stillness.

The hooved animals were moved out of Pets Corner and after three weeks a decision was made to open the Zoo with all precautionary measures remaining in place. The first visitors were greeted with whoops of excitement from the chimps and the gibbons once again started their chorus.

2001 will be remembered with horror at the disastrous effects on the countryside and the farming and tourism industry.

TWYCROSS ZOO

PLEASE HELP TO CONSERVE WILDLIFE

The daily work of running Twycross continues, benefiting wildlife with studies in Conservation, Research and Education – subjects covered fully in the Mission Statement published each year in the Annual Report.

However, this would all cease without funding. Twycross, although a Charity, depends entirely for funds on income derived mainly from gate receipts. We do not receive any Government grant. If you would like to help the work further – either by Deed of Covenant, a Legacy or just a straight donation – please contact the Zoo Office of Twycross Zoo, at Atherstone, Warwickshire, CV9 3PX.

Index

Molly Badham has been keeping primates and other animals for nearly fifty years. She is currently co-director of the Twycross Zoo East Midland Zoological Society.

Maureen Lawless is a double award-winning journalist, who has written for a wide variety of publications on animal issues, including *News of the World*, *Daily Mail* and *Mail on Sunday*. She runs the Bromsgrove branch of The Farm Animal Sanctuary; the first sanctuary set up specifically to provide a home for sick and injured farm animals, which she co-founded in 1986.